Oui!

Parisian Secrets for a Dream Wedding

Text and illustrations
by Delphine Manivet
with Anne Akrich

Flammarion

*For my daughter, Brune, with whom I hope to share
the magic of my profession, and the meaning of love,
of celebration, and of the sacred—
that ineffable sense of eternity
that makes life more beautiful and more joyful.*

*To my son, Adam, may he know
the benefits of love and become—
if not Prince Charming—a good man.*

Contents

Introduction

I'M DELPHINE MANIVET and, for more than sixteen years, I have designed thousands of wedding dresses and attended hundreds of ceremonies. In the course of working with all of those brides-to-be, I recorded, in 372 notebooks, their reflections, beauty advice, wellness tips, and love stories, with all of the doubts and difficulties that come with them.

I also received nine marriage proposals! That makes me a bona fide expert, doesn't it?

Okay, enough with the swagger—let me tell you where my fascination with marriage comes from. When I was eight years old, my mother, a social worker in Nice, took me every weekend to wander around the flea market where she worked. One day, I stumbled upon a wicker suitcase. When I opened it, I was amazed at the treasures inside: a collection of pretty, delicate things, period lace, a card from 1920. I didn't know it at the time, but it was a bride's trousseau—a time-honored tradition that consists of gathering objects and accessories linked to the future bride's roots and heritage. They thrust me into this imagined stranger's life, and I was fascinated. I instinctively recognized the joy, beauty, and tradition that these items represented. It was the loveliest thing I had seen in my short life and would be a guiding light throughout my life.

When I was twenty-one, I left my home in the south of France to enroll in fashion school in Paris. I was full of dreams and felt like the luckiest girl alive, living in the most beautiful city in the world.

But things really clicked for me when it came time for my own wedding. After receiving three proposals as a young woman, the fourth was "the one," and at the age of twenty-six, I embarked on the great nuptial adventure. My first obstacle: the wedding dress. There was nothing I liked. Nothing. Well, of course there was haute couture, but a Valentino dress that cost six figures just wasn't an option. So, I resolved to design my own dress. Using the vintage lace from the trousseau I had found as a child, I made a wedding dress for the first time—my own. After that, I began designing dresses for my friends. And that's how I got started.

In the eyes of Parisian women, wedding dresses are seen as somewhat unfashionable, weighed down with the expectations of tradition. When I began making my own creations, wedding dresses were still considered rather kitsch and unstylish; people still equated them with sugared-almond colors and clouds of tulle and ribbon. The challenge was to make wedding dresses chic. I viewed this as an opportunity to offer a new perspective and bridge these two historically separate worlds: the cool of fashion with the sweetness of marriage. I created my brand by following this very natural path.

My profession allows me to observe different expressions of femininity and societal evolutions. Case in point: even though I mainly address women in this book and most often refer to the heterosexual couple, I have witnessed all forms of love, and have helped to celebrate many same-sex marriages. Simply put, my book is for everyone. For practical purposes, I use the words "men" and "women," but they encompass everyone who wants to love and who seeks to give meaning to their love. I always try to imagine how the marriages and celebrations of tomorrow will look.

Marriage is like a book, and the wedding is the first chapter in your shared story. It must be written with care, and conceived in terms of meaning, breath, phrasing, and style, to find your own voice and follow the path that best suits you—the one that will express your unique character and make your wedding one of the most beautiful stories of your life.

More than just a survival guide for the bride-to-be, this book is a collection of women's wisdom, a testament to sharing and love. It celebrates Parisian elegance and chic, as well as the distinctive culture of French romance.

édition limitée

Robe courte
edwardienne
"Paulin"

Dentelle de Calais.

des reins !

Mt en
biais

Satin
double
mousseline
crêponnée

Sous robe

sans
couture

Delphine
Manivet

THE *PARISIENNE*

I moved to Paris at the age of twenty-one, when I decided to follow my dreams and study fashion design.

By taking that step, I was now within reach of this fantasy, this ideal, this mirage that shimmers in the distance like the Evening Star, this model of femininity envied around the world: the *Parisienne*! Who is she? What does she do? How does she do it? What is the secret to her confidence and air of mystery? What happens in her bedroom, in her dressing room, in front of her mirror?

The *Parisienne*—the Parisian woman—is above all a construct. I realized at a very young age, when I began traveling, that this image has a very strong impact and global reach. But her reputation can be divisive: when I returned home to the south of France, I was labeled "la Parisienne" with more than a hint of disdain. For the rest of the world, however, the Parisian woman is the exemplar of French elegance. I have many international connections, including a store in London and retailers all over the world. Because I travel a lot to see my clients, actresses, and models, I'm able to observe the differences between countries.

I think I can safely say that, today, when I talk about the *Parisienne*, I'm talking about myself, as well as my friends and my brides. I claim this concept as an integral part of my work and my life.

The *Parisienne* is a French icon, like champagne or croissants. She guarantees a form of elegance, a style, an indefinable je ne sais quoi—but if you try to pin down this special something, you may get lost along the way.

Her essence is not easy to define, in any regard. She can be compared to a reflection on the water's surface: the closer you get, the harder it is to make her out. A successor to Marie Antoinette, the courtesans of the Belle Époque, and the feminists of the twentieth century, the *Parisienne* carries within her the history of these proud, soigné women who defined and defied fashion. In fact, the very word "fashion" comes from the French expression *à la façon de*: in the eighteenth century, women ordered dresses *à la façon de*, or in the style of, Marie Antoinette. It was not so much the sumptuousness of the fabric that mattered, but the way it lay on the body. The Parisian woman has inherited this essential savoir faire. She knows how to put together an outfit in a certain way, to combine styles to create a unique and distinctive appearance.

Liberated, independent, and creative, the Parisian woman appears to be many things without actually being any of them. She cultivates the art of "seeming." She seems natural and gives the impression of having just slipped into a pair of jeans and a sweater, while she actually thinks about her style a great deal. Everything is considered. She has a form of detachment, self-discipline, and modesty. Men appreciate this, of course, but so do women, who try to copy this air of effortlessness and mystery.

This poise is in her DNA: she doesn't give herself away or ever fully reveal her secrets. She always manages to keep up appearances. She never lets herself go and is always in control. Even when having a good time, she keeps it together.

Everything is a question of attitude. The *Parisienne* gives the impression of having a great deal of self-confidence and being at ease in any situation. She masters the subtle combination of chic and chill, of casual and put together. Comfort is very important to her—she has to feel at ease. Wearing suitable clothing enables her to cultivate an inner nonchalance, and she will look appropriate whatever the time of day, without having to change between a morning meeting and an evening drink with friends.

She has a very particular relationship with beauty and self-care. She is comfortable with her differences and turns

them into strengths, knowing how to highlight her unique features. The description of the celebrated actress Sarah Bernhardt springs to mind, with the director of the Théâtre de l'Odéon famously saying, "She was not pretty, she was worse." In the same way, the *Parisienne* does not succumb to standardized ideas of beauty; she is capable of creating charm from what others might consider flaws. She looks to strong role models that give her confidence. In my case, I was named Delphine because my mother greatly admired the actress and director Delphine Seyrig, and she wanted to pass on a little of her strength through this name.

When it comes to seduction, people outside of France see the *Parisienne* as an expert in love and joie de vivre. When my clients work with me, they feel like they are claiming a bit of this legendary sensuality and magic for themselves.

In their view, she exemplifies French style. Chic and polished, she delivers the "wow" factor. My clients strive for the kind of easy elegance that her style embodies. They want to tick all the boxes: not just the dress, but also hair, makeup—the whole package. In a way, they want to distill the essence of the Parisian attitude and appearance. As for the "French kiss," it still makes me laugh when people ask me how to do it!

I

THE PROPOSAL

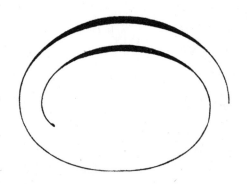

We're Getting Married!

THIS IS IT: you've said "yes" to the love of your life. The most beautiful journey is about to begin—but it's also a path strewn with obstacles that sometimes can be grueling and difficult. So how do you take those first steps? And most importantly, what questions should you ask before setting off?

"WILL YOU MARRY ME?"

I often ask my brides to tell me about their proposal. Their responses vary widely: for some, it is a spectacular event, for others a very simple one. In some cases, the bride is the one who proposes; in others, the couple broach the subject during an otherwise ordinary conversation. But these moments always carry something of the eternal and sacred.

Marriage proposals occupy such a special place in the collective imagination because they are rooted in very old traditions. For example, in medieval Europe, when receiving a knighthood, the recipient knelt before his lord. Kneeling when making a proposal is a continuation of this custom: a sign of devotion and respect, but also— and above all—a sign of loyalty.

Whether your significant other has pulled out all the stops or simply popped the question, now is the time to savor the moment. You will have time to think about organization later, even if it is tempting to start drafting the guest list or gauging the length of your train.

In reality, the most important, and maybe the hardest, part of all is finding the right person. You might get it wrong, but it's never too late to reconsider! Planning a wedding is one thing, but it has to be with the person you want to spend your life with. You know you've found them when being with them makes you a better version of yourself, when you grow and learn. Of course, love is defined by the feelings you have for each other, but it is also based on your capacity to love yourself with your partner's support. Take a moment to ask yourself if your partner:

- Brings you breakfast in bed from time to time
- Does whatever they can to help you solve your problems
- Has organized a surprise dinner or party for you
- Has a job you don't hate
- Pays attention to the children in your life
- Gives you an orgasm
- Gives you multiple orgasms
- Naturally smells good to you, even when they sweat
- Asks you a lot of questions. (Face it, if they don't, they aren't very interested in you.)
- Carries your luggage and holds the door for you. (To be honest, this one is far from a deal-breaker, it just appeals to my old-fashioned side—I love chivalry!)
- And finally, do you sometimes prefer to be without this person? (This is a trick question—the answer should definitely be yes! It is healthy to have separate interests.)

Most importantly, relax—these are just guidelines! Ask your own questions, or don't ask any at all. Let yourself be surprised and trust life. My best friend is about to marry a man who doesn't meet any of the criteria she initially set out for herself. She dreamed of marrying a tall, strong man with a beautiful head of hair, but her fiancé is short and bald. Love has the power to surprise us and introduce us to new things—and I'm not just talking about lack of hair.

The Ring(s)

WEDDING RINGS ARE THE SYMBOL of a pact that unites two people, the material sign of a sacred moment, whether the marriage proposal or the ceremony itself. Traditionally, there are two rings: an engagement ring and a wedding band.

As with other parts of the wedding ceremony, things are changing when it comes to the rings, but if I had to give some advice, it would be that the wedding band should be thin, elegant, and discreet. It could be a simple, delicate, threadlike ring or a band studded with diamonds.

As for the engagement ring, it can be flashier and embellished with a larger, round or cushion-cut stone. Some popular styles today are inspired by vintage or art deco pieces.

Typically, both the engagement ring and the wedding band are worn on the left hand, but in some countries, the engagement ring is worn on the fourth finger of the left hand until the day of the marriage, when it is moved to the same finger on the right hand and replaced by the wedding band. This tradition is based on an Ancient Egyptian belief that the left "ring" finger is directly connected to the heart by the *vena amoris* or "vein of love."

According to tradition, your partner should propose to you by presenting a ring in a small box. But times are changing: many couples choose a ring together, to make sure it's the right size, or to the bride's taste. Some brides choose their wedding band on their own, buy it themselves, make it, design it, or even purchase a new one several years later. Others make the choice not to wear one at all.

The *Parisienne* has a special relationship with her engagement ring and wedding band, one that breaks with the rules of the past, and is governed instead by a kind of creativity and expressive freedom. She has no qualms about wearing her rings on certain days and not others, removing her engagement ring now and then, or wearing it in unexpected ways.

The secret is to find a ring that suits you and that tells a story. Looking to the past or to tradition may help you give new meaning to whatever is important to you. For this reason, it can be useful to know about the symbolism of precious stones when choosing a ring. Although white diamonds are popular in Paris, I have noticed more and more of my clients expressing a desire for something more distinctive by choosing a colored stone.

THE MEANING OF PRECIOUS STONES

DIAMOND .... *union, commitment, eternal love*

EMERALD......... *hope, regenerative power, true love*

SAPPHIRE .... *purity, wisdom, faithfulness*

RUBY ....*strength, passion, sensual love*

AMETHYST...*devotion*

MOONSTONE ....*innocence*

PEARL...*love*

TURQUOISE..............................*memory, true love*

CORAL .... *confidence, courage*

I am always touched when people show me their ring, explaining, with a combination of pride and modesty, where it came from and the story it tells.

I personally have received nine marriage proposals and seven rings. (And I still have them all—well, no one asked for them back!) Here's a brief rundown of what I've been offered:

- three intertwined gold bands
- a micro-diamond on a gold band
- a round white diamond on a platinum band
- a black diamond on a jade band
- small sapphires and microdiamonds
- a ruby on a silver band
- small diamonds set in rosettes on an engraved ring
- a suggestion to get matching tattoos on the inside of our ring fingers in place of a band (I declined, but it's a fun idea)
- a champagne wirehood

If I were to ask a man to marry me today, I would give him a flat band in engraved white gold set with a micro-diamond inside. And if I were to ask a woman to marry me, I would give her a nearly transparent ring of diamond micro-beads.

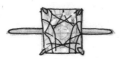

II

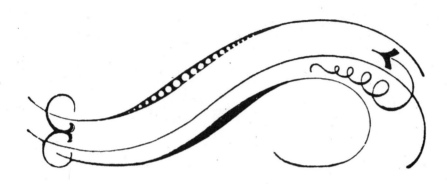

IMAGINING
THE PERFECT
WEDDING

Finding Inspiration

NOW THAT YOU ARE READY to take the plunge, you find yourself facing a blank page. Where do you begin? How do you start creating the most beautiful day of your life?

First of all, consider what will be at the heart of your wedding, what you would like your guests to remember about this day. What unites you and your significant other? What values do you share? Are there any childhood dreams you want to make come true? Taking time to reflect on these things will help you lay the framework for your ceremony and set aside anything that isn't right for you. If you are committed environmentalists who lead a simple life in harmony with nature, there is no point poring over photos of designer bling.

You don't have to bury yourself in stacks of books and magazines or frantically pace the aisles of wedding fairs. Your marriage cannot be everything at once: you risk drowning in the tide of advice available online and in the hundreds of publications devoted to the subject. Instead, choose what matches your taste, your story, and your personality. One step at a time, you will build your own personalized list of references.

In the first few weeks, let the inspiration soak in: write down what strikes a chord and discard those things that, upon reflection, don't really speak to you; make mood boards in a notebook or on Pinterest. The structure of your wedding will gradually take shape according to the direction that you choose.

The Theme

WHEN YOU THINK "WEDDING THEME," incredibly kitsch or saccharine images may come to mind and send you running. You don't *have* to choose a theme, but if you want to, consider it as a common thread that can help you make decisions and tell a story.

For example, you could choose a theme related to the place where you are having the ceremony (it doesn't make sense to have a city wedding with a bucolic theme or a desert wedding with a seaside theme). The trend today is to think local, so don't count on shipping in lavender from the south of France, for example, unless that's where you are getting hitched. Show consideration and respect for the environment where the celebration will take place, all the while trying to make it shine. Make the most of your surroundings, and don't try to fit a square peg into a round hole.

Choosing a theme also gives you the opportunity to pick a color scheme for your wedding. Unless you're a color expert, focus on a limited range of shades. You can start with your—and your fiancé's—favorite colors or compose a palette based on the ambience at the reception venue.

These five themes with a French accent can be adapted to your own venue:

- *Guinguette*: on a riverbank, strings of lights, checked tablecloths
- Traditional brasserie: oysters, champagne, waitstaff in long aprons
- Vintage Belle Epoque: nineteenth-century style, generous buffets, vintage tablecloths, candelabra
- Art deco–1920s: wine served in small vintage crystal glasses, guests in velvet coats or flapper-style dresses and tuxedos
- Versailles-inspired: peonies in champagne buckets, Billecart-Salmon bubbly, fine porcelain

The Ceremony

NO MATTER WHAT FORM the ceremony takes or the meaning it holds for you, it will be the event that sets your wedding celebration in motion. Often emotionally intense, the ceremony itself may bring together a small, core group of loved ones or all of your invitees. When it comes to the ceremony, the golden rule is to choose the format you are most comfortable with—the one most consistent with what is important to you and your partner.

To make your union official in the eyes of the law, you must complete the obligatory administrative procedures where you live—and they vary according to local practices. Whether you decide to mark the occasion with a civil and/or a religious ceremony will be determined by local regulations as well as the traditions and beliefs you and your partner hold. In France, the legal steps come first and take place in *le mairie*, or city hall, where the bride or groom (or their parents) live. A religious ceremony may also be held in a place of worship on the same or on another day followed by a reception. Obviously, it makes things easier if the reception takes place not too far from the ceremony, but you can always work something out. You might have a very small ceremony in the city hall or special place of worship, with just a few of your closest friends and family, and then hold a large reception on another day.

Religious ceremonies tend to heighten emotions: in one family, there may be an uncle who refuses to set foot in a church or a grandmother who refuses to consider the marriage valid if you don't go before a priest. Some couples may not share the same religion. Do whatever *you* as a couple want. Getting married in a church or under a chuppah or before an imam is meaningful if you and your partner feel a deep connection, in whatever way, to the religion in question. There are many ways to include your families' stories in your wedding. Keep an open mind and honor the people who are dear to you, but don't let yourself get caught up in something that you aren't comfortable with.

Another solution is to hold a secular ceremony. This format is very popular because it allows you to create your dream wedding from scratch—to get family and friends involved, to perform symbolic gestures, and to exchange meaningful vows—I can assure you, there will be tears! If you choose this option, you will need an officiant. Depending on the country, it might be a justice of the peace, magistrate, registrar, or licensed celebrant. A friend may speak in an unofficial capacity, but they cannot legally marry you unless they also happen to be ordained.

How far in advance you need to reserve a place of worship or venue varies greatly, depending on the location and time of year, but it is not unusual to have to book a year in advance. For popular venues and destination weddings you may need to plan further ahead still. If you want to say "I do" in a popular wedding spot (like Paris!), you'll need to build in even more time.

Choosing the Reception Venue

THE WEDDING RECEPTION is an opportunity to get creative. You could plan an extravagant picnic in a meadow with large, low tables and cushions on the ground, jars of candles scattered everywhere, and a piano in the grass; or a sumptuous dinner in a manor house, grand hotel, or château, complete with table service, antique silver candelabra, and a string quartet; or a cozy gathering at an inn with a warm fire in the hearth and a local band setting the tempo. What is most important is to find a place that you like and that tells your story.

For my first marriage, we chose a lovely vineyard in the south of France, with a chapel and a pretty cloister: it was exactly what we were looking for and a good match for our large number of guests. We wanted to celebrate late into the night, and the remoteness of the location made that possible. This is important to consider: the owners of many venues impose a cut-off time—particularly if it is a historic building—and will shut down the party if it overruns.

If I were to remarry, I would look for something simpler and more intimate, perhaps a romantic museum or a typically Parisian brasserie, where oysters and champagne would be served.

The theme may inspire your choice of menu or vice versa. But what I like most of all are offbeat choices, invention, creativity, and playing around with tradition. A Louis XIV theme on a barge or in a garden can be very effective. Be adventurous!

Setting the Tone: Style and Venue

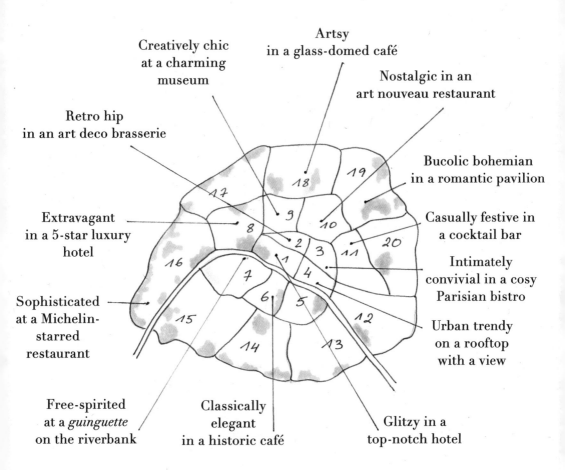

Creatively chic
at a charming
museum

Artsy
in a glass-domed café

Nostalgic in an
art nouveau restaurant

Retro hip
in an art deco brasserie

Bucolic bohemian
in a romantic pavilion

Extravagant
in a 5-star luxury
hotel

Casually festive in
a cocktail bar

Intimately
convivial in a cosy
Parisian bistro

Sophisticated
at a Michelin-
starred
restaurant

Urban trendy
on a rooftop
with a view

Free-spirited
at a *guinguette*
on the riverbank

Classically
elegant
in a historic café

Glitzy in a
top-notch hotel

The key to celebrating your wedding in a style and setting that feel "just right" to you and your partner is to get creative. The above tour of Paris offers a variety of ideas for adding Parisian flair to your reception. You can set a tone that is classic or hip, sophisticated or bohemian, artsy or glitzy, and then scout out venues that will create the ideal backdrop for your unique celebration.

The choice of venue plays a crucial role in determining the rest of your budget. If you put all of your money into booking a wonderful location, you may not have much left over for the rest. It's always better to serve champagne and delicious food in the backyard rather than potato chips in a palace!

How far in advance you have to reserve will depend on the type of space you choose: a fashionable restaurant, the garden of a museum, a family home, a fairytale castle, or a picturesque farm — contact the places you have identified as soon as possible as you may need to reserve a year or more in advance.

LE JARDIN ET L'HOTEL DE M. POIRET
(A LA FIN DE LA 1002' NUIT)

LA PARISIENNE
DE PARIS
L'AISE DE
L'EXPOSITION
1900

PRIX NET 1 fr.

GALERIE VERO-DODAT

CAFE DE L'EPOQUE

MAISON FONDÉE EN 1826

CAFE DE L'EPOQUE

LE TRIOMPHE
DE LA
PARISIENNE

NOS CONCOURS

The Guest List

WHEN IT COMES to establishing the delicate subject of the guest list—your families, friends, your friends' children—conventions have changed a lot over the years. Today, the rule is to do what you want. A new trend of "mini-weddings" is emerging. Taking this approach means you can reduce the number of guests without offending loved ones (or, in any case, leaving them less offended than if they had been excluded from a large celebration). The couple should follow their hearts and their instincts, and avoid putting added pressure on themselves. Ultimately, the goal is for everyone to be happy.

Use the following equation to draft a guest list:

The wedding party
+ children (if you have any)
+ close family
+ friends (if possible, split equally among the couple)
+ a few of your parents' friends (if you are under 35)

Don't forget about each guest's plus-one (or more). If you have trouble solving this complex equation, sit down with your partner and draft your ideal guest list. If it's too long, make a second list in priority order.

SHOULD CHILDREN
BE INVITED?

This is an important question. Inviting the children of family and friends represents a considerable expense, and you need to plan something to keep them occupied and accommodate their dietary needs, so everyone can enjoy the big day. The wedding should be fun for them, too. (You don't want to put them off, or they may not want to get married themselves one day.)

If you don't have the budget, explain to your friends honestly and simply why their children are not invited. If you tell them you have decided on a smaller, adults-only wedding, they'll understand.

That being said, children bring joy to a wedding. The tradition of the ring bearer and flower girls (the *enfants d'honneur,* in French) is still very important. Children from the couple's family are given priority, then the children of friends. The bride buys their outfits. They are expected to prepare the bride's entrance by strewing the ground with flower petals and holding her veil or train to make her comfortable. They also hand out the rice that is thrown as the married couple exit the ceremony. Historically, the children in the wedding party have played a role of recognition for the families, enabling everyone to find their place.

Bridesmaids and Witnesses

HAVING BRIDESMAIDS is an ancient tradition. It's a nice way to let your close friends know that you love them. Traditionally, young, single women were chosen to be bridesmaids so they could find a sweetheart during the celebration, but there are no set guidelines in this regard.

On the big day, the bridesmaids—led by the maid or matron of honor—help make the wedding festive: they add to the excitement and provide support to the bride-to-be. They look after her bouquet, veil, and train, help her get ready, and attend to her before and after the ceremony. Bridesmaids may also encourage guests to dance during the reception.

There are no rules when it comes to how many bridesmaids you should have, but between three and five is a good benchmark. In a church wedding, they stand to the left of the bride. It is customary for their bouquets to be inspired by the bride's, but smaller.

Depending on local regulations, one or more witnesses may be required to certify a marriage. For a civil wedding in France, each partner must choose at least one and at most two witnesses (the future spouses do not have to have the same number of witnesses). Witnesses can be family members or friends. Their main role is to attest before the officiant that your union is genuine, but they are also people you can rely on during the ceremony. Along with the other members of the wedding party, they will help your family and friends get into position for the ceremony, gather the telephone numbers of guests to inform them in case of delays, look after the rings, move flowers, bring the newlyweds' car around, and more.

They also play a very symbolic role. On the day of the wedding, they will remain by your side, supporting you when emotions run high and bringing you whatever you need.

Asking a loved one to be a witness is also a celebration, an event that seals a bond—it's a special moment to cherish. You can accompany your request with a gesture such as a handwritten letter, a charm, a small gift, or a keepsake.

MY ADVICE

When a witness is required, he or she must bring some form of ID to the ceremony so the wedding can take place. Otherwise, someone else will have to step in.

You may find it easy to choose your maid of honor or witness. But if you have several very close friends, the decision may be more difficult.

I suggest choosing someone who you think will be able to reassure you on the big day. If one of your friends tends to worry or, on the contrary, is ultra laid-back, this might not be the right role for them.

As always, make the choice that feels right. You can involve your other friends in different ways, for example by inviting them to be a bridesmaid or to take responsibility for a specific task.

ADVICE FOR YOUR SINGLE BFF

Finding true love always looks easy from the outside, but there are some essential steps before a wedding can take place: meeting someone; mutual desire; falling in love; getting to know their family, friends, pets, and colleagues; discovering their habits and fears. During this formidable journey, it's important not to excuse poor taste, excess, criticism, and missed dates. Once the proposal comes and the whirlwind of planning begins, the effort it took to get there can often be overlooked—even by those closest to you. Keep in mind that the wedding may bring up mixed emotions for those who have not yet found true love. To ensure your single BFF doesn't get discouraged and is able to fully support you on the happiest day of your life, here are some common-sense dating tips that *Parisiennes* apply:

- You arrive at a party, you see him, you're drawn to him—nothing could be more elementary than this law of attraction. The dance of desire is about to begin. Don't rush toward him with desperation in your eyes. Observe from a distance with a "Marilyn" gaze, smile, and keep your movements slow and controlled. Even if you're churning inside, try to stay calm, and simply let your presence flood the room with light.
- On a first date, avoid piling on accessories—you're not a Christmas tree. Focus on what suits you, on what makes an impression. One of the keys to feeling confident is to find a go-to outfit that you can put on without thinking. People often imagine the *Parisienne* wearing a trench coat, a little sweater, and boots. The reality is, she has adapted to her environment. Paris dictates her style. One of the unique features of this city is how easy it is to move from one ambience to another in a matter of minutes. Clothes that are simple and comfortable, yet chic, let you adapt to any

situation. Your date outfit can be a simplified version of what suits you best.

- The secret to being beautiful is to feel good in your body and to be proud of it. It's not easy to see ourselves how we really are. Look at yourself in the mirror kindly and gently; try to observe any minor flaws with a new perspective—you might be able to turn them into advantages.
- Women have been fighting for autonomy for centuries and continue to do so today. Make it clear that you are independent, that you have your own life, friends, family, passions, interests, tastes, and job. All you ask is that you learn from your date and that he learns from you. From this balance, a harmonious relationship can emerge.
- Avoid sending a stream of texts. The perfect message is a question that invites the other person to respond in some way. Take a pause and think before sending the text you've just written. Certain things are best kept to yourself. Don't write and share everything that goes through your mind.
- Try to avoid passive-aggressive comments and cynical remarks. Treat the words you give or receive with great respect.
- Emotions may run high, but you can learn to control them. Try to welcome them in your body before expressing them. When we are overwhelmed by our feelings, other people are rarely able to understand the internal tsunami we are experiencing. Our emotions belong to us, they are the result of our history. No one else is responsible for them.
- Don't try to glom on the other person at all costs. If they have plans or want to leave, don't throw your arms around their neck, pleading with them to stay. Put yourself in their shoes—it's unbearable.
- Don't cling like a barnacle.

- In the beginning of a relationship, avoid conversations that are clearly about marriage. On your second night out, don't grill your date between the cheese course and dessert to find out his true intentions. Sound him out, but stay discreet.
- Beware of inopportune "I love you's." Say it rarely, but with feeling.
- Don't ask for constant demonstrations of love. It may be tempting, but it's a burden for the other person to constantly have to prove their feelings. Remember that if you're together, it's because they love you. If you need to be reassured (it happens to us all), rather than asking for a declaration, say, "I want to spend more time with you. I'd like to go out to dinner together this weekend." You'll get much better results.
- Try not to criticize their friends or family. Even if a cousin with dirty nails is a little too fond of guns for your taste, refrain from making judgments about the people in their life.
- Don't spend all your time nagging. Pick your battles—you always have a choice. Don't pretend to be happy if you're not, but if that's the case, think about finding a new partner.
- If they hurt or offend you, never try to hurt them back—it will always backfire. Revenge is the worst thing you can do to yourself. Don't waste time trying to make the other person jealous on Instagram. A content woman doesn't have time to post photos of her happy life on social media.
- Argue, a little. Unfortunately, I'm a pro at answering "nothing" when my partner asks me what's going on, even if something's wrong. I need to remind myself that it's okay to disagree. Trying to prove you're right has never made anyone happy. I've been thinking a lot about how to argue more calmly. Ideally, we should

communicate our feelings authentically, speaking from our own point of view, without attributing thoughts or intentions to the other person.

- To be happy in a relationship, you have to feel comfortable in your own company. To get married, you have to want to marry yourself. That's the starting point. In fact, that's how you should think about it. Marriage is not a life raft. It's a new space where three parties co-exist: you, your partner, and your relationship—the third entity that you create to grow, improve, and eventually form a family together.
- There are as many expressions of sexuality as there are couples, so don't feel guilty about anything. I'd love to say I have relevant advice that applies to everyone, but the fact is, I don't hold the secret to burning desire. So good luck to each and all!

Budget and Timeline

THE WEDDING BUDGET is a sensitive matter. The total varies enormously depending on the kind of ceremony, the location, the couple's style preferences, and individual financial means—and the cost varies widely from country to country, region to region, and household to household. It really comes down to the couple's financial situation. Although it was considered customary for parents to pay for their child, today there are all manner of ways to foot the bill. Tradition once dictated which family covered the reception expenses—for example, the bride's family typically was responsible in the United States or Australia, while the groom's family paid in China and France. In recent decades, it became the norm for the families of the bride and groom to share the total. Nowadays, with people marrying later, or having more than one marriage, the bride and groom often pay for the wedding themselves. A modern approach is for each set of parents to pay for their friends, while the bride and groom pay for theirs. This last solution generates the least amount of guilt and helps to ease the stresses related to managing the wedding finances.

I suggest that you discuss the budget early on and as openly as possible. Draft a simple table to evaluate costs. Work out an amount per head for catering, broken down to include food and alcohol. Determining a budget for each category will give you a fairly accurate idea of the grand total. The pie chart on the facing page offers a guideline for balancing how you allocate your overall budget. Once you have an estimated total, simply divide that amount by the number of guests to reach a per-person budget. This will enable you to easily divide costs between families, if that is what you are

Budget Breakdown

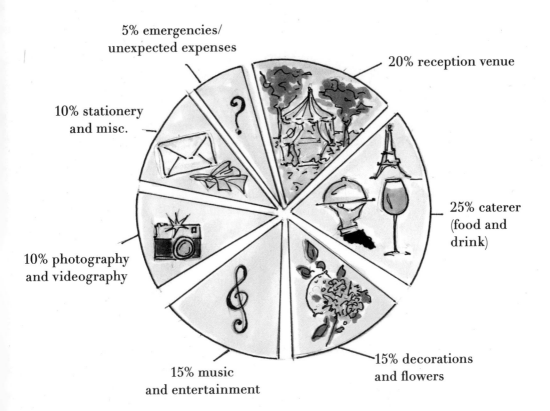

5% emergencies/ unexpected expenses

10% stationery and misc.

20% reception venue

10% photography and videography

25% caterer (food and drink)

15% music and entertainment

15% decorations and flowers

planning to do. Of course, if financial situations vary greatly, the breakdown can be adjusted accordingly.

To lower the budget, either reduce the number of guests or the duration of the reception.

Usually, the bride and groom or their family pay for everything related to food and drink, but not guests' accommodation or transport. Occasionally, the couple will cover the cost of local transportation and accommodation for close friends and family and the wedding party. In any case, they send, by email or with the wedding invitation, a list of accommodation near the venue that covers a range of budgets. Bear in mind that your wedding will represent an expense to your guests. Have the consideration to suggest various alternatives, from simple bed-and-breakfasts to five-star hotels (for those who can splurge).

Another French tradition called for the bride's mother to pay for her daughter's dress up to the age of thirty-six, while the bride's aunt or grandmother provided the veil. Today, the French bride usually buys her own dress. If her mother wants to contribute, she might offer jewelry or an accessory.

It is just as easy to lose track of time as money when planning a wedding. Getting started about a year ahead should give you a comfortable timeline.

Get the Bachelorette Party Started

ONCE YOU'RE ENGAGED, you can host a gathering to announce the big news to the people who will be invited to the wedding. The engagement party can be as simple as a meal in a restaurant or an intimate evening event.

The bachelorette party or hen night takes place several weeks before the wedding. The tradition of bidding adieu to single life appears to date back to the eighteenth century, but at the time was solely reserved for men. It amounted to visiting a brothel, usually in an advanced state of inebriation, and was a way of "educating" the groom-to-be in his conjugal duties. The purpose of the ritual has completely changed today, with women adopting a modern version of it around the 1960s and 1970s.

The bachelorette party is usually organized by the maid of honor and bridesmaids. The bride rarely plans it herself.

My advice: keep it elegant. A typically Parisian bachelorette party might include a chic lunch followed by a spa day with girlfriends, or an evening at a restaurant with dancing. Male friends can also be invited—times have changed and conventions are not as strict as they once were.

The bachelorette party should reflect the bride-to-be's personality. This shared moment is a time to celebrate and honor, not ridicule, her. There's no need to play humiliating games or go skydiving. However, there will be much laughing, dancing, love, and champagne!

P.S. A bachelorette party is not shorthand for throwing self-restraint to the wind. Don't: rent a limousine with "Bride-to-Be" scrawled all over it; dress the future bride in a pink sash and shiny tiara; force anyone into a ridiculous costume—or invite a stripper. That's a definite no!

The *Parisienne* doesn't vomit in her hair at her bachelorette party, so forget the vodka shots and tacky underwear—stick to moderation and composure to create a memorable event.

Spotlight on Riley Keough

ONE OF MY MOST VIVID MEMORIES is of a dress that I created for Riley Keough, Elvis Presley's granddaughter. It was wild to be in Nashville, in a stunning family home, surrounded by three generations of women: Elvis's former wife Priscilla, their daughter Lisa Marie, and granddaughter Riley.

The day before we met, I found myself in a typical Nashville bar surrounded by Elvis impersonators, and I realized just how strange the whole situation was.

When I went to their home, there was a strict protocol to follow and dozens of bodyguards. Everything I had with me was searched, all the fabric samples and dresses—it was very intimidating. I had been told that I shouldn't speak to the Presleys too much and that I should avoid eye contact. I'm not a "fangirl" type, and I intended to follow the rules without giving it much thought. The reality was that their simple, generous welcome put me right at ease. I was standing before any other mother and grandmother about to marry off their daughter and granddaughter. In fact, I ended up spending Christmas there. It was wonderful, and it will always be a special memory for me.

Riley is one of the most charming young women that I have ever met, and the love she continues to show for her husband is pure and inspiring. I count myself lucky to have been able to participate in her big day and to bring a touch of Parisian elegance all the way to Nashville.

III

GETTING
GORGEOUS

The Dresses

THE WEDDING gown should tell the story of the woman who is getting married: from the little girl and the young woman she once was, to the woman she is now and the one she will be some day. The challenge is finding the delicate balance that represents her and that she will continue to identify with years from now, when she reminisces about her wedding day. My best advice is to ask yourself if the dress you have chosen will always be "you" when you look at your photos in decades to come.

My greatest responsibility is to convey my client's story through her dress. This is a very personal process. The dress must reflect the complexity and layers of identity that make a woman who she is. That is why the right dress is so hard to find.

White wedding dresses are a relatively recent phenomenon. Queen Victoria started the trend in 1840. Before that, women from more modest backgrounds simply got married in their best dress or in a vividly colored one—red, pink, blue, brown, or even black—because it was less expensive to have colorful or patterned garments made and it was complicated and expensive to keep a white dress clean in the era before washing machines were invented.

MY TRIPLE-S RULE

THE WEDDING DRESS should be:
    Simple
          Spectacular
               Sensual.

Designing dresses that are both simple *and* spectacular has always been my goal, and it's a difficult one to achieve. These two concepts may seem contradictory, but they inform my notion of beauty and elegance. It is much easier to create a dress covered in flounces and embellishments than a simple, sublime sheath dress that could reveal any flaws in the fabric, cut, or assembly.

For a simple dress to be beautiful, it must be perfect. And by simplicity, I also mean readability. To tell a story well requires only three elements: an introduction, an evolution, and a finale. The same is true for a dress—a simple narrative thread makes an impact and a memorable garment. If you add more elements, you lose the essence; if you omit one, the dress becomes nondescript. For example, a wedding dress can't have lace, a bow, embellished buttons, pearls, and frills all at once. It's too much—the story gets muddled. You should be able to describe the dress in three words. For example, a satin dress could have an open back, a bow, and small, fabric-covered buttons. That's it—there shouldn't be any other noticeable attributes. To me, simplicity is the ultimate form of sophistication and the aim of my work.

By "spectacular," I mean striving for that "wow" factor. Most of us want to make an impression at our wedding (otherwise we would just wear sweatpants). We hope to make an impact: first, on the person we're marrying, but also on our guests. When we walk into the room, we want hearts to soar. The wedding gown is unique—it has to turn heads. This search for the extraordinary lies at the heart of its design.

Finally, the dress has to be sensual. To me, sensuality should be implied, not flaunted. In the collective imagination, this is one of the *Parisienne*'s innate talents: she suggests without displaying. Sensuality lies in small details like a cuff or a neckline—which doesn't have to be plunging. The dress should hint at a woman's curves, not exhibit them to the world. In the nineteenth century, women covered their necklines with panels of lace called *modesties* in French. Today, modesty remains an art to be cultivated.

The fabric must also be sensual. Be sure to touch and become familiar with the material; it should be a second skin. Some women love the feel of satin, others find it unappealing. Some find comfort in muslin, others in cotton. The connection between the fabric and the body is part of what makes a dress beautiful. Be very careful when choosing a gown based on a photo: some polyesters look wonderful on paper or online, but are awful to the touch. You have to think about how you'll feel in your dress, but also the fact that you will be in contact with dozens of people who are going to hug and kiss you all day long.

In the past, young French women often wore small hats or headdresses with ribbons fluttering behind them, called suivez-moi-jeune-homme *(follow-me-lad). These floating strands were a light-hearted invitation, a discreet way of signaling that a woman was available for courtship. I often place a ribbon or bow on the back of my dresses as a nod to the* suivez-moi-jeune-homme, *because I find this tradition so moving.*

 MY ADVICE

1. Keep the big picture in mind. It would be a shame to wear a beautiful dress with hair that overshadows the gown and ends up being all that anyone remembers. You have to strike a balance between the dress, hair, makeup, and accessories.

2. Strive to look your best when trying on wedding dresses at the store. Wear good-fitting undergarments similar to your skin color, and bring a pair of heels the same height as the ones you plan to wear on the big day.

ANATOMY OF A DRESS

The rule of three also applies to the structure of the dress, which should not have more than three horizontal lines. For example, if you wear a bustier gown with a pronounced waist and a ribbon, you shouldn't wear a necklace—it would throw things off and the ensemble would be unbalanced. Always think in terms of lines.

The Perfect Fit
The shape of the body's muscles
trace dynamic lines.
The lines of the dress should follow
at least three lines of muscle contours.

WHERE TO FIND A WEDDING GOWN

1. A wedding dress designer. The budget may run ten times and up compared to a ready-to-wear dress—a custom-made or haute-couture dress would cost significantly more.
2. Ready-to-wear. Many brands now offer lovely and affordable white dresses.
3. Rental. Some establishments offer a rental service with prices varying depending on the dress.
4. Second-hand. If you're not superstitious, certain websites specialize in pre-worn (only once, naturally) wedding dresses, where you can find gowns for half price, or even less.
5. Vintage. Why not get married in a genuine 1920s wedding dress? You may have to find an experienced tailor to make alterations on what may be fragile fabric, or even replace certain elements, but it will be one of a kind.

If you plan to get your dress from a designer or a specialist shop, the first fitting should ideally take place eight months to a year before the wedding day. And if you order a dress that you can't try on in advance (from a website, for example), do so far enough ahead of time to find something else in case it doesn't meet your expectations.

DO	DON'T
• Attend fittings alone, with a male friend, or a close confidante — perhaps your chief bridesmaid — but no one else	• Attend fittings accompanied by five friends
• Remember to bring pretty undergarments when you try on the dress — ideally the ones you plan to wear on the big day	• Give into clichés (I'm tall, so I should wear a tight, strapless bustier dress; I'm small, so I should wear something short; I have large breasts, so I should show them off)
• Imagine your dress in thirty years time	• Try to look like someone else
• Find the right shade of white or ivory	

BRIDESMAIDS' OUTFITS

It has been customary, since at least the 1920s, for bridesmaids to dress alike: originally this was to make it easy
for eligible bachelors looking to identify potential mates.
Nowadays, I don't necessarily recommend matching bridesmaids' dresses, for the simple reason that they will all have
different body shapes. However, it is possible to agree on
a theme, a color, a print, or an accessory that will work for
everyone.

In some countries, the bride pays for their dresses—
in fact, in the past, it was the only thing she was directly
responsible for. Whenever possible, I think it is gracious to
do so, rather than forcing your friends to bear the cost. When
possible, the *Parisienne* buys the bridesmaids' dresses and
shoes, or at least one of their accessories.

It's All in the Details

"Choosing an accessory requires extreme care—a kind of mathematical precision. It is of the utmost importance, and there is no room for error."
Maggy Rouff, *La Philosophie de l'élégance*, 1942

THE RULE OF THREE

In the 1920s, fashion designer Jean Patou used the word *riens*, or little nothings, to describe scarves, gloves, bags, perfume, and other accessories—a subtle way of suggesting that they are, on the contrary, everything.

Accessories must be chosen with care. The *Parisienne* always applies the rule of "less is more." Coco Chanel once said: "Before you leave the house, look in the mirror and take one thing off."

As a matter of course, apply the rule of three: if you choose a distinctive pair of shoes—sequined or with bows, for example—they become a separate accessory. The veil is also an accessory, as are eye-catching earrings.

OLD, NEW, BORROWED, BLUE

Your wedding day is also an opportunity to honor a delightful tradition that originated in England. Following the traditional rhyme, to bring good fortune, the bride must wear:

something old	something new	something borrowed	something blue

This custom provides an opportunity to involve women from your family, or other women close to you, in the preparations. The *Parisienne* appreciates this kind of humble, non-religious tradition that unites women across generations.

The "something old" symbolizes the bride's connection to her family over the ages. It is often a piece of family jewelry but could also come from the groom's family or from a female friend. It might be a lovely vintage veil or pair of gloves, antique embroidered tablecloths placed on the reception tables, or silver candelabra or cutlery used as table decorations. I particularly like the idea of attaching to the bouquet an antique locket containing a photo of a departed loved one. It is a nice way of connecting generations and honoring the person's memory.

The "something new" represents everything that will be created through marriage, and also symbolizes success and abundance. Often the bride's dress fills this role, but it could also be her shoes or a pretty set of lingerie for the wedding night.

The "something borrowed" is intended to bring luck and happiness to the newlyweds. Tradition dictates that it should be borrowed from a happily married female friend, but you could just as well ask for something from anyone else you love. It could be a piece of jewelry, like earrings, a locket, or a bracelet that belongs to your grandmother or your mother, or a friend's veil. I like the idea that this borrowed object reflects your relationship with a woman close to you and represents your bond. You could plan something special for the moment she gives it to you.

The "something blue" represents fidelity and purity within the couple. Often this is a discreet item: a handkerchief with the couple's initials embroidered in blue, a sapphire ring or pair of earrings, a pale blue silk kimono the bride wears while getting ready, or blue-gray velvet heels, for example.

I've revisited this tradition by sewing a blue mother-of-pearl button into the lining of my dresses. In the past, dressmakers would stitch a strand of their hair into the lining of wedding gowns to bring the bride wealth and babies. It's the intention behind the design that makes a wedding dress beautiful.

Ideas for the Traditional Four Items

Something old	Something new	Something borrowed	Something blue
vintage jewelry	wedding gown	veil	handkerchief embroidered with blue thread
antique tablecloths for the reception	shoes	jewelry belonging to your best friend	sapphire
a vintage kimono for the bride to get ready in	lingerie	the recipe for your favorite cocktail	blue kimono
			blue velvet shoes

88

Shoes

THE MOST IMPORTANT thing to consider when choosing a pair of shoes is posture and gait. There is nothing glamorous about hobbling down the aisle. If you've never worn high heels in your life, don't choose your wedding day to try them out—you won't be graceful. Wear whatever you are used to wearing—what you can wear with ease. Women who are used to walking in 6-inch (15-cm) heels can absolutely wear them on their wedding day, but if that's not you, then it's a really bad idea. It is wise to wear a heel of some sort, however; even low heels accentuate the curve of your lower back and result in a slightly slower gait.

Comfort is essential on the big day. Remember, as the bride, you will almost never sit down. You will be in high demand and your feet sorely tested. So, pack two pairs of shoes: stunning heels for photos and the beginning of the ceremony, and something comfortable to slip into later for dancing.

French brides are not against going barefoot. If the wedding takes place in summer near an ocean, the bride might end up barefoot in the sand. This can be a sensual experience—and fun—but bear in mind that your feet will be on display.

My advice is to skip sandals with a long dress, or you may not see anything but your toes. A better option is a pair of pointed or round (or something in between) closed-toed shoes. Nude, ivory, and white are all suitable colors, but shoes should always be a shade darker than the wedding dress, never lighter. If you wear an ivory dress, for example, don't wear white shoes. I suggest wearing heels between 2–4 inches (5–10 cm). Heels measuring 2½ inches (6 cm) and over should be narrow; anything lower can be a little thicker.

However, if you wear a midi or short dress, you can really get away with anything, from strappy sandals to closed-toed shoes. The only mistake would be trying too hard to match your shoes to your gown. If you choose a lace dress, avoid lace shoes; velvet, suede, satin, and leather are all good options. Your accessories don't all have to coordinate or match your dress. Instead, the idea is to create balance, and to express your personality through your outfit from head to toe.

If you wear a short dress, you can accessorize it with feminine double-strap sandals, a reliable classic. But keep an eye on the number of lines that structure the overall look. The goal is to make your feet appear as small, chic, and as "invisible" as possible.

RECOMMENDED HEEL HEIGHT

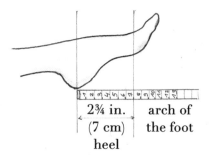

2¾ in.   arch of
(7 cm)   the foot
heel

Sit and extend your foot, letting it relax comfortably. Measure the distance between the ball of the foot and the back of the heel to calculate the recommended heel height.

CALCULATE YOUR IDEAL HEEL HEIGHT

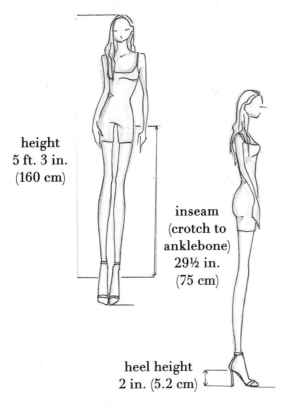

height
5 ft. 3 in.
(160 cm)

inseam
(crotch to
anklebone)
29½ in.
(75 cm)

heel height
2 in. (5.2 cm)

1. Convert height and inseam from inches to centimeters by multiplying inches by 2.54
2. Calculate ideal heel height: (height [cm] / inseam [cm] − 1.61) × 10 = 5.2 cm (2 in.)

Also, the idea that shoes get "broken in" over time is false. If a pair doesn't feel comfortable when you try them on in the store, there's a good chance they'll be equally uncomfortable on your wedding day. We all have different feet and arches, so testing shoes before the big day is essential. Even if you think a pair is gorgeous, if they don't feel good, bid them *adieu*.

In the nineteenth century, the courtesan Lola Montez wrote in her book The Arts of Beauty, or Secrets of a Lady's Toilet: *"There is a delightful promise in a fine foot and ankle that the rest of the limb is shaped with the same exquisite grace.... But there is a remarkable charm in a walk characterized by blended dignity and vivacity. It leaves upon the beholder a lasting impression of those attributes of mind which most surely awaken esteem and admiration."*

MY ADVICE

New shoes are often slippery because the soles are completely smooth. Score the bottom of your shoes with a pair of scissors—ideally seven diagonal cross-hatch marks—before wearing them. They will grip the floor better and keep catastrophe at bay.

Jewelry

JEWELRY SHOULD BE WORN in moderation. I generally advise my clients to wear a pair of earrings: either small cultured pearls—as Coco Chanel said, pearls are makeup for the skin—or diamonds, very fine gold or silver hoops, or lever-back earrings to illuminate the face.

The idea is to add glints of light to the outfit, but jewelry should not be conspicuous unless it is among your three chosen accessories. There's no need to hit the stores in search of something to wear around your neck—once again, it's a matter of lines, and a necklace might add an unnecessary one to a dress. In my opinion, a bare throat and shoulders are ravishing on their own. You can wear a necklace if it goes really well with the gown and if you prefer it to earrings, but it's a choice you have to make. When you leave the ceremony, you will already be wearing a wedding band, so according to the rule of three, that leaves only two accessories left to choose.

MY ADVICE

Don't wear a bracelet on your left wrist. That's the side the rings go on, and it should stay uncluttered and elegant, especially on the day of the wedding. You have your entire life to pile on the jewelry.

The Bridal Veil

THE TRADITION of the bridal veil dates back to the Romans. The future bride wore what was known as a *flammeum*, a large scarf made of lightweight organdy, which was considered a bearer of good omens. In some cultures, the bride's face was completely covered by the veil, as a way of keeping grooms who had never seen their betrothed from leaving before the union had been sealed. What nerve!

In the Middle Ages, the bridal veil was made of several layers of linen, a far cry from the tulle used today. It was attached with small threads of gold, which represented wealth, and was supposed to protect the bride from the evil eye.

Personally, I have always loved the veil, which I think is the greatest symbol of the bride. I like the tradition in France of draping your bridal veil over your baby's crib for good luck; this cherished keepsake can be used to signify a parent's protective love for their child. I often tell my brides about this tradition, and they love the idea.

Parisian Veils

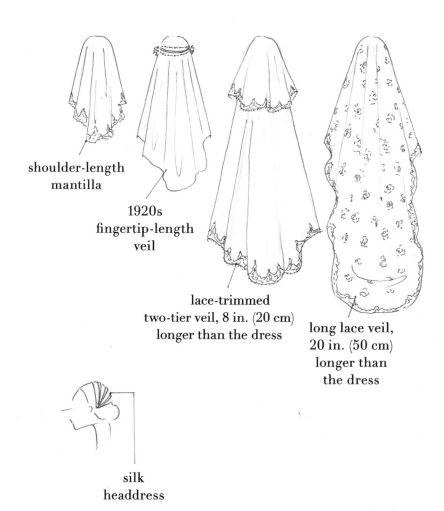

shoulder-length
mantilla

1920s
fingertip-length
veil

lace-trimmed
two-tier veil, 8 in. (20 cm)
longer than the dress

long lace veil,
20 in. (50 cm)
longer than
the dress

silk
headdress

Nowadays, many women don't want to wear a veil, but since I really like this part of the trousseau, I have been coming up with alternatives since I first started out. I created a little lace top that evokes the idea of modesty and is meant to be taken off after the ceremony, like a bridal veil. Another option is to wear a very small veil, such as a flyaway veil or a birdcage veil, or a flower in your hair.

Bridal veils are often made of lace-trimmed silk tulle. Others are made entirely of lace (in France, the best come from Calais or Caudry), or simple versions in ivory or white tulle. The veil can be the same shade as the dress or slightly darker, but, like the shoes, it should never be lighter.

Lingerie

IT'S TIME to retire a cliché: no one should wear sexy lingerie on the day of their wedding. Undergarments should be comfortable, flattering, and, most of all, invisible. There's nothing chic about underwear showing through your wedding dress. To be completely undetectable, it should be the same color as your skin, so don't just choose a shade that you thought looked good on a model. This is a basic, but very important, point.

MY ADVICE

On the big day, go without a bra for at least four hours before the ceremony; these instruments of torture could leave unsightly marks on your skin that take time to disappear.

The Bouquet

THE BOUQUET shouldn't be too big. An enormous one tends to take up a lot of space in photos and hide the bride—it's all anyone sees, making it a main character when it should remain an accessory. Flowers can also be very heavy. The bride will have difficulty carrying her bouquet with ease and elegance if it weighs five pounds.

MY ADVICE

Avoid embellishments—lace is the worst. Think: simple, simple, simple.

A typical Parisian bouquet is small, round, and "country chic." A nice touch is to add something to a bouquet that tells your story: for example, a sprig of mimosa if you're from Nice, wisteria if you were born in a small English village, or a protea flower if you have South African origins. The bouquet will be all the more elegant if it evokes memories.

The rule of three also applies to the bouquet. Never combine more than three flowers, and keep foliage to a minimum—it adds bulk to the arrangement. The flowers I often recommend to my brides-to-be, depending on the season, of course, are sweet peas, peonies, hydrangeas, roses, cherry or plum blossoms, and lilies. I also like orange blossom, which represents fertility and purity, and myrtle, which was once considered a sacred flower and symbolized Venus, the goddess of love. Learning about the language of flowers can be a way to invest each element with meaning. You'll find many books on the subject. In the past, wedding announcements were often decorated with symbolic plants: daisies for innocence, ears of wheat for fertility and wealth, forget-me-nots for true love, laurel leaves for love's victory, mistletoe for kisses, oak for strength, pansies to mean "thinking only of you," roses for all aspects of love, or thistles for the pleasures and pains that come with love.

Floral arrangements for the wedding can be different from the bride's bouquet, but linking them through a common element or two creates visual cohesion.

The key to creating an elegant aesthetic is to choose flowers and foliage in keeping with the place where you are getting married. Building a theme around olive trees can be very chic if the wedding is being held in Provence, but much less so if it is being celebrated in Norway. Stay true to yourself and tell your own story!

Composing a Meaningful Bouquet

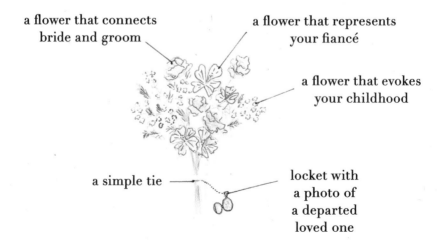

a flower that connects bride and groom

a flower that represents your fiancé

a flower that evokes your childhood

a simple tie

locket with a photo of a departed loved one

The tradition of the bridal bouquet has existed since the Middle Ages, when women would make bouquets of orange blossoms, appropriately symbolic for their wedding day. At a time when few people could buy ointments or perfume, carrying these fragrant flowers was also a way to smell good.

In the past, the size of the bouquet was an indication of the scale of the ceremony. An enormous bouquet in a period photo suggests that the wedding was lavish and sumptuous. It was a sign of wealth and social standing.

Hair

ON THE WEDDING DAY, your hair should be immaculate and elegant, but it doesn't have to be swept up in a triple chignon if that's not your style. My advice: be cautious about trying anything new. Test your hairstyle before the wedding day, whether or not you decide to work with a stylist. Personally, I think brides should learn to do their own hair with the help of friends, unless they plan on having a traditional marriage with a lot of fanfare, and they want to bring in their usual hairdresser.

Hair is an essential part of the bride's ensemble and is central to the final result. If it isn't just right, it can ruin the overall look. The lines of the hairstyle should follow the lines of the dress, so whether you decide on a bob, a ponytail, or loose locks, everything should be proportionate. Hair trials are best done once you have chosen the gown, or at least the main features, such as straps, a round neckline, a bustier, or an open back. A good technique is to have your hair done by a skilled stylist, take photos, then review them with photos of the dress to see if the looks work together.

Hair should be washed the day before the wedding, never the day of, so that it stays in place better. The Parisian bride often goes for natural waves: her hair is texturized and lightly curled in different directions to create a typically Parisian "tousled" look. Her look tends to be soft, not too controlled. She might choose a loose up-do, or a more "undone" style, such as leaving her hair down with a few strands pinned up, or a chignon with a few wisps of hair framing her face. A low chignon with a part down the middle is an elegant classic that creates a beautiful ballerina look.

Don't put too many things in your hair, like shiny barrettes, tiaras, or other accessories. However, depending on the season or the type of veil you're wearing, you could add a fresh flower. As a general rule, choose a simple, natural-looking style.

Most importantly, stay true to yourself. If you have curly hair, it would be a shame to straighten it for your wedding day. In that vein, stay away from risky experiments, like giving yourself bangs for the big day if you've never had them before.

A wedding hairstyle should be part of a whole. You don't need dozens of individual mood boards for your hair, dress, and shoes—a mood board is only useful to show how everything works together. Find a balance between the elements in your outfit, keeping in mind that your hairstyle plays an integral part of it.

Bridal Chignons

high bohemian   ballerina   half-moon   loose bohemian

1970s style

105

- One of the best hair tips I ever received came from a friend's aunt who lived in India, in the Himalayas: everything comes down to brushing. Invest in a high-quality brush with natural bristles. Brushing your hair removes impurities without the need for shampoos and serums than can irritate your locks, while also tightening the cuticle layer and stimulating the scalp. She also recommended rinsing until the hair sort of "squeaks"—a sign that it is totally clean. I still follow this method. Even before washing my hair I brush it well, then fully wet it before applying shampoo.
- If your hair is very dry, apply a serum or lemon juice and wrap it in a towel to dry.
- Perfect your look with a toothbrush. Put a little hairspray on the bristles to tame flyaway hairs. It might seem a little strange, but this technique works wonders.
- Another tip: dry shampoo can be used to texturize hair and easily achieve a wavy look. Plus, it smells good.

DO	DON'T
• Get color or highlights done at least three weeks before the big day • Use dry shampoo • Rinse hair with cold water to revitalize the scalp and tighten the cuticle layer	• Get extensions • Wash your hair every day

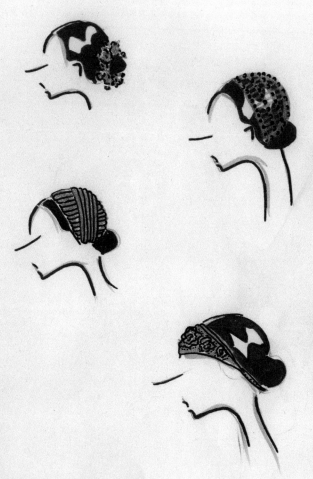

Delphine Manivet
COUTURE

Makeup

THIS IS ANOTHER AREA where you should avoid the unknown on your wedding day, so test everything ahead of time. While some women dream of getting their hair and makeup done by professionals, my advice is to keep things simple and do it yourself. If you don't have a trusted cosmetologist, it's best to do your own makeup or ask a friend who has a flair for it.

Remember that the wedding day is an emotional one. There will be a lot of kissing, and you will probably cry, so avoid applying too much foundation—if you wipe away the traces of your aunt's lipstick from your cheek, you may end up with unsightly gaps. Opt for natural makeup tones—pink, peach, or coral—and wear a similar nail color. Try to steer clear of anything flashy.

MAKEUP MASSAGE

It is essential to prepare your skin before applying makeup.

Start with three brushes:
- *Use a wide, flat brush to apply your eye cream.*
- *Use a round fluffy foundation brush to apply a rich moisturizer to the driest areas of your face, which usually extend from the sides of the jaw to the temples. Don't forget to apply it around your eyes and nose.*
- *Finally, using a fluffy, flat brush, apply an anti-shine primer to create a matte finish and tighten pores. Focus on the T-zone, which includes the lower part of the forehead, the space between the eyebrows,*

the inside corners of the eyes, the eyelids, the area around the nose (but not the bridge), the area around the mouth, and the chin.

Then, with a clean toothbrush reserved for this purpose, and ideally one with a wooden handle, vigorously brush your eyebrows and comb your eyelashes.

Using lip balm, massage your lips from the outer edge inward, including the inside of the lips.

Using your finger, apply a bit of cream blush to the top of your cheek bones, eyelids, lips, upper forehead, chin, and tip of your nose.

If the makeup massage is done well, it may be all you need before heading out the door.

The day before the wedding, you can use a facial scrub and mask, then massage your skin with a serum before applying moisturizer. My secret is to let the moisturizer soak in for a few minutes before applying makeup. That way, you can see where shine-prone areas are sufficiently hydrated and blot them with a cotton ball or small makeup sponge.

There are no hard and fast rules when it comes to makeup. We all have different faces, so get to know yours— observe yourself and learn to balance your own proportions, if needed.

I am a big fan of "no-makeup makeup." It's great to let freckles show and let naturally thick eyebrows be themselves.

The *Parisienne* wears little to no foundation. She prefers to use moisturizer and a bit of concealer, concentrating on areas where she has small imperfections, like under the eyes or around the nose. To immediately brighten the face, you can put a hint of lighter concealer on the outer edges of your eyes, where small red fatigue lines sometimes form, or at the corners of your mouth, which can form shadows.

But this implies finding the right concealer—one that most closely matches the color of your face. However, your complexion is made up of several shades, which is why you shouldn't cover your face in a uniform layer of foundation, at the risk of creating a "cakey" effect. Try to have at least two shades of concealer: one for correcting imperfections and another for brightening.

NATURAL MAKEUP

Bronzing powder and blush are French makeup essentials. If you have a naturally beautiful complexion, you don't need anything else. Rather than "contouring," the *Parisienne* usually prefers to use bronzer to subtly make a large forehead look smaller or a wide chin narrower.

The *Parisienne* doesn't use a lot of eye shadow. If she does wear it, she uses a blending technique to keep it natural, rather than reveal the effort that goes into creating the look. Mascara or a thin stroke of eyeliner is fine. I often use clear brow gel on my eyelashes to hold the curl.

Eyebrows can be subtly sculpted with tweezers, but I always urge my daughter to use this tool sparingly: if you pluck your brows too often when you're young, they may not grow back later. You don't want to lose the structural density that helps define your face. However, you can lighten your eyebrow color by one or two shades, at most, which can significantly soften your facial features.

Observe your face when applying makeup, especially your hairline, which is often asymmetrical. This is easy to see in a three-way mirror. Our hairline considerably influences the shape of our face. Smooth down the hairline with a toothbrush to find what you like best.

PARISIAN GLAM

The Parisienne's *secret weapon is her ability to perfect a no makeup look that lets her natural beauty shine. I call this "Parisian Glam," my preferred makeup style.*

After your makeup massage, use a fluffy brush to apply concealer between your eyebrows, on the bridge of your nose and the area around it, the outer edges of your eyes, the bow of your upper lip, the corners of your mouth, and your chin. Then use a very small detail brush to focus more specifically on imperfections.

Use a makeup sponge to apply transparent setting powder to your T-zone and jawline.

Next, use a large brush to apply bronzing powder to your neck and jawline, the top of your cheekbones, and the upper part of your forehead.

Comb your eyelashes, then curl them and apply clear mascara. Then apply black mascara only to the outer lashes of your top lids.

Apply peach-, rose-, or light brown-tinted eyeshadow to your lids; the browbone should remain open and clear. Brighten the inner corners of your eyes with a touch of highlighter.

Using a brown eye pencil, on the outer third of your lid, draw a very light line along your top lash line,. Do the same for the lower lash line.

Using a subtle liquid highlighter, place a tiny drop on the bridge of your nose, sweep it downward, and use the excess on the top of your cheekbones and your browbones.

Finally, if you like, apply a slick of lipstick and blot with a tissue. Don't worry: I'll tell you exactly how to find the shade that best suits your face.

MY ADVICE

- A friend of my mother's gave me an excellent tip regarding lipstick. She made her own and always looked exquisite. Her secret: find the shade closest to the color of your nipples. This tip has a long history: I also found it in a book written by the nineteenth-century courtesan Lola Montez. Our bodies are well designed; we just have to learn to observe them. I've tested this advice with many of my friends and it never fails. Getting the right color usually requires mixing two or three shades; you'll rarely find it in the store.
- Use this same hue on your cheeks and eyelids. And, to give yourself a radiant complexion—such as after a workout, or a day spent skiing or outside in nature— use it on the tip of your nose, the upper part of your forehead, and your chin, places where the sun would naturally color your skin. This creates an impression of freshness and good health, which is perfect for your wedding day.
- Create touches of light on your face, using one of the many excellent highlighters available on the market. Apply a dot to the top of your cheekbones, the center of the Cupid's bow, and the bridge of your nose. This will capture and reflect the light that naturally falls on these areas.
- Your eyes will be their most beautiful when you smile with your entire body, soul, and heart. This intention, and the sentiment within, will light up your eyes naturally. When you smile this way, you say "I love you" without uttering a word.

- Every woman should have a good eyelash curler. It requires a small investment, as plastic models can really damage eyelashes. Avoid devices that heat up, too. Women with very few lashes can apply false ones, but use only one or two on the outer part of the eye. Never use the whole strip.
- Invest in a range of good brushes—they will last a lifetime. You can do anything with the right tools. Using brushes to apply facial products also helps the skin absorb them well.

DO		DON'T
• Have a professional lighten or darken the shade of your eyebrows according to your complexion • Invest in an excellent eyelash curler		• Tattoo your eyebrows • Use a dark liner pencil to excessively enlarge your lips • Apply a lot of foundation

Preparing Your Body

YOUR WEDDING DAY is approaching and you want to have the body of your dreams—to be your most beautiful self on the big day. You plan to go on a diet, do a cleanse, or swallow magic potions, all to look ... like *what*, like *whom*, exactly?

DIETS

Since I started in this business, I've seen women from all backgrounds try various approaches to reach an ideal on their wedding day. I think I've figured out what works and what doesn't. Some women try diets that essentially involve starving themselves: single-food, high-protein, or liquid regimens, or even total fasting. In my experience, it doesn't work, or at least, not for long.

The *Parisienne* follows a much more effective diet that I call the "regeneration" diet—it's all about aligning body and mind. As she prepares for her wedding, the bride-to-be is under a lot of pressure; she doesn't have time to think, and she tends to be stressed. The challenge is to get the body to function as intensively as the mind in order to achieve inner calm. Only physical activity can achieve this balance. I highly recommend Pilates, especially for women who aren't used to exercising.

In other words, prioritize slowness. That's the guiding principle of this book and my main invitation to you. A mindful diet plan for a mindful wedding: get back in touch with your body and give it a break.

What I have found works best for me is intermittent fasting, which I follow quite naturally. With this method, the body is allowed to rest and rejuvenate; it needs calm and a break from producing energy in order to digest correctly. (Note: A lot of research is available on the benefits of intermittent fasting, but it may not be for everyone. Check with your doctor if you have underlying health conditions.)

A good way to start is to not consume any food between 11 p.m. and 2 p.m., for example. In fact, this corresponds to the lifestyle of the Parisian woman; she is often content with an espresso for breakfast. Her day is a slow build-up of energy, creativity, and social engagements. When she lingers with her girlfriends over an apéritif or dinner, she takes her time. After work, she doesn't stand at a bar chugging a beer. Take a leaf from her book: if you're going to have a drink, enjoy it. Sit down and make it a moment to enjoy with friends or a celebration. Sharing is essential to Parisian *art de vivre*. In the same way, when the *Parisienne* dines, she sits down and has a conversation. This approach to meals plays a major role in keeping the *Parisienne* slim. She doesn't snack. In fact, the French in general don't simply eat—they lunch or dine.

One of the best tips I've ever received came from a grandmother who lived in the south of France, in the hills around Nice. She was extremely flirtatious and very beautiful. The first thing she did each morning was to rinse her mouth with olive oil. She believed that, during the night, the body works to release anything that isn't good for it, anything too heavy to digest. These fluids accumulate on our tongue, in our nostrils, and even in our eyes, finding their way out via our natural orifices. We often hear that the first part of any beauty routine should be to drink a tall glass of water in the morning; she believed that would simply flush back inside everything that the body spent the night trying to eliminate.

Of course, we don't always have the option to use olive oil every day. But a thorough warm water rinse of the mouth, nostrils, and eyes, or a swish of mouthwash is also very effective.

Soulful Chicken
Bouillon Soup

For two small bowls: boil the equivalent of two bowls of water. Add one chicken bouillon cube and half of one vegetable bouillon cube, a small amount of vermicelli, and a pinch of coarse salt. Sprinkle with coriander. Lower the heat and stir occasionally, with a lot of love, until the vermicelli is cooked.

Top with shredded cheese and garlic croutons, if desired.

What the *Parisienne*
Orders in a Restaurant

- If she needs comforting: onion soup, a small plate of fries, and two glasses of white wine.
- If she feels she should watch her figure: a plain omelet with side salad, a Perrier with a slice of lemon, and an espresso with no sugar.

The No-Crumb
Diet

Here's an effective and easy-to-remember tip: avoid all foods that leave crumbs, such as bread, croissants, and cookies.

DO

- Sit down for meals or when having a drink, and celebrate these moments
- Practice intermittent fasting
- Use mouthwash in the morning
- Practice Pilates or yoga
- Take care of your microbiome: during the pandemic, we lost much of our bacteria because we lived in an antiseptic world; I recommend getting out into nature and letting things take their course

DON'T

- Starve yourself
- Fast for long periods
- Go on a single-food diet
- Snack
- Drink a bottle of rosé—or any color wine—on your own

SKIN

Everything begins and ends with the skin. I've noticed that, in anticipation of the big day, many women are prepared to go to extreme lengths, including injections, Botox, and all the rest. I cannot discourage this enough. Even if it's just a new scrub or cream, don't try anything unfamiliar the day before your wedding. If you want to test something different, do it at least fifteen days before the event: you never know how your skin is going to react. The only treatment you should do the day before is a gentle face and body massage. At this point, you can forget about anything that includes artificial or self-tanning, or cosmetic procedures.

On the day of the wedding, you could start with a Finnish massage, then apply a little moisturizer to your face, arms, and legs—but not to your chest, shoulders, or stomach. Your skin shouldn't be too hydrated in the areas where your dress lies closest to your body, to avoid transfer. You can apply talcum powder there, however. Above all, avoid high-shine creams or oils, which inevitably cause sweating and slippage.

The Finnish Facial Massage

I learned this technique from a friend, an artist from Helsinki. The Finns have been practicing it for generations. Contrary to current trends, which recommend using rejuvenating stones or serums, this facial massage relies on the fingers only. Anyone can do it (see p. 122).

The Finnish Massage

Interlace your fingers,
then place your hands over your eyes

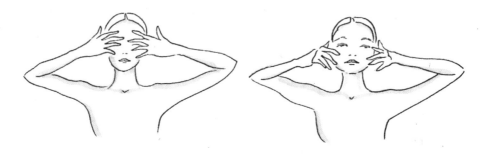

Apply gentle pressure, then slide
your hands with fingers extended
towards the sides of your face

If your skin is still red in certain areas (between the eyebrows, at the corners of your mouth, around your nose, or on your chin, for example), it's a sign of dehydration. Continue stimulating these areas with the stretching massage until the redness fades. And hydrate!

• This first tip comes from my Finnish friend. Finns take a holistic approach to the body and beauty, and many have houses near lakes, where they go to feel restored. In winter, they alternate between dips in frigid lakes and sessions in the sauna. My friend explained that we are encouraged through advertising campaigns to hydrate our skin with creams day and night, when it really isn't necessary. Our skin already has everything it needs to renew on its own. Continually slathering our skin with products makes it lazy, she argues—it "forgets" how to take care of itself because we don't let it. Her solution was a three-day "nothing" cleanse. I tried one with her in Finland. We went to the sauna and the lake, and did nothing else. My skin felt a bit tight at first, but the feeling soon faded. Natural hydration and suppleness return very quickly. I don't think my skin has ever been as beautiful. I do this cleanse whenever I can: either during a stay in the country or in Paris when I have a bit of downtime. After a three-day break, my skin looks radiant again.

• Another wonderful bit of advice comes from the courtesan Lola Montez. In *The Arts of Beauty* (1858), she explains that you should have a small white towel for your face and a medium-sized towel for your body. The idea is to keep water from drying on the skin, so Lola advises vigorously rubbing dry your face, neck, and body. The bath towel is therefore an essential beauty tool, and it should always be clean. After drying, you can massage your face to prepare it for treatments. Friction has been one of the greatest beauty secrets since the eighteenth century, and—having practiced it myself for years—I can attest to its effectiveness.

- My grandmother passed on to me her love for Elizabeth Arden's 8-Hour Cream. It's the only one I use, and I always take it with me when I travel. An extremely rich moisturizer, it soothes everything from burns on children's skin to scratches to chapped lips. It's the fountain of youth in a cream. Sometimes I put a thick layer of it on my face before bed and in the morning my skin looks magnificent. It's been around for ages, and the scent might take a bit of getting used to, but every woman should have some in her bathroom cabinet.
- A final piece of common-sense advice: sleep whenever you can. The *Parisienne* doesn't get up at four in the morning to do yoga, drink detox juices, and answer emails before cleaning her apartment. Sleep is one of the greatest beauty secrets of all.

Skin Care Routine

Morning
- Rinse your face with cold water
- Using a cotton ball, apply micellar water
- Do a Finnish massage using a light oil or vitamin-rich serum
- Massage behind your ears—they hold up the lower part of your face
- Apply a day cream, ideally one with SPF
- Perform the makeup massage (see pp. 109–110)

Evening
- Rinse your face with warm water
- Use a foaming cleanser
- Do a Finnish massage with Elizabeth Arden's 8-Hour Cream

DO	DON'T
• Perform a Finnish massage every morning and evening	• Get Botox just before the wedding
• Use a facial scrub once a week	• Use facial scrub daily
• Use self-tanning wipes	• Use a tanning bed
• Dry your face with a white face towel	
• Periodically, leave your face free of products for at least two days	
• Moisturize behind your ears	
• Drink water before bed	
• Get enough sleep	

Throat and Décolletage

When we're young, we often overlook moisturizing our neck, cleavage, and breasts. And yet, these are among the areas that show signs of age the fastest. Don't skimp on hydration!

DO	DON'T
• Practice regular breast massage: using the palm of your hand, massage in a counterclockwise motion to foster lymphatic drainage and bolster appearance	• Have plastic surgery several weeks before the wedding (beware of scars)
• Use your face cream on your chest	• Exfoliate your breasts
• Apply talcum powder to your breasts on your wedding day, especially if you're wearing a strapless bra	• Sleep in a bra
• Go without a bra four hours before the ceremony to avoid marks on your skin	

TEETH AND SMILE

It goes without saying that nothing conveys happiness like a beautiful smile. And healthy teeth always brighten up a face.

DO	DON'T
• See an orthodontist	• Get veneers
• Gently whiten your teeth	• Have optical whitening (it damages tooth enamel)
• Brush your teeth and gum line in the morning, after every meal, and before bed	
• Floss	
• Clean your tongue with a tongue scraper every morning	

HANDS AND NAILS

The *Parisienne* takes a simple, minimalist approach to her nails. They are always well groomed, well filed, and on the short side.

On her wedding day, her nails will be plain, transparent, and almost pink. Forget long nails, nail art, and diamanté—stick to something simple.

My grandmother gave me some sound advice: there is no universal nail shape—you have to find the one that best suits your hand. Square nails may look good on one person's hand and oval nails on another's. Trends should not come into play. To find the shape that best suits you, file your nails when they're polished—ideally with a dark color so the skin underneath doesn't influence what you see.

As a general rule, finger- and toenails should be polished with the same color (or in similar shades). Your entire appearance should be unified—nothing should cause the eye to linger besides the areas you have decided to highlight.

Your feet and ankles also deserve care—they are a very sensual part of the body. Rub down your feet well with a towel when you get out of the shower, and don't overlook any areas, including between your toes. Before bed, you could also apply rich moisturizer or shea butter to your feet, then cover with a pair of socks, resulting in baby-soft feet the next morning. Consider doing this several days before the wedding, especially if you plan to wear open-toed shoes. Looking elegant "from head to toe" did not become a figure of speech without reason.

I suggest getting a manicure and pedicure two or three days before the wedding. For impeccable polish, however, apply it the day of the event. Very pale peach, coral, or ballet-slipper pink are all good options: you want a subtle effect. The *Parisienne* doesn't go for "statement" nails!

How to Select the Right
Shade of Polish

Just as for your lips, you can use your skin tone to find the color that is most suited to your nails. A shade might look fabulous on one woman and bland on another, so you have to determine if your skin contains more yellow, orange, or red undertones.

At the store, hold the bottle of polish up to the inside of your wrist. This way you won't be confused by the creases in your knuckles or by skin that may be flushed by heat or red from the cold.

How to Apply Polish

- Gently buff your nails
- Coat them with a rich moisturizer
- Wipe them with a cotton ball soaked in very hot water to soften your cuticles
- Push back your cuticles using a cuticle stick
- Apply a base coat
- Apply a first coat of polish, starting from the center
- Wait until it is dry, then apply a second coat of polish
- Finish with a top coat of speed setter

Protect Your Hands

- Apply moisturizer several times a day
- Wear kitchen gloves when doing housework
- Wear gloves in winter to protect your hands from chapping

Maggy Rouff was a celebrated fashion designer in the 1910s. She wrote a beauty manual, La Philosophie de l'élégance, *that I have owned for many years. In it, she writes that she kept cooled wood ashes in a small jar and rubbed them on her nails to remove the streaks and stains that can form with age. I've done this several times and it works incredibly well. It also brightens cuticles.*

DO	DON'T
• File your nails to the shape that flatters your hand; keep them short and trimmed	• Get false nails
• Use polish in a natural, rosy hue	• Get a French manicure
• Push back your cuticles using a dedicated tool and/or a gel	• Cut your cuticles
• Just like for your skin, periodically leave your nails free of product for a few days	
• Apply sunscreen to your hands to prevent age spots	

Spotlight on Lily Allen

LILY ALLEN is one of the most memorable brides I've worked with. At the time, she was the UK's sweetheart, single-handedly representing a new style of rebellious rock'n'roll, and people loved her. She was quite eccentric and unreserved, but on her wedding day, she was determined to be a "normal" bride, to join the great community of married women.

When she came to my boutique, she loved looking at the names and sketches on the garment bags waiting to be shipped. She told me she was eager to become "one of them."

The traditional side of marriage was important to her, and she especially wanted a French-style wedding. As for her dress, she gave me carte blanche. I sketched a gown for her in Calais lace, paired with a 1920s veil; she loved it immediately.

I didn't know it at the time, but many celebrities have several dresses made by different designers and then make their choice on the day of the wedding. Lily had a gown designed by Karl Lagerfeld at Chanel, but she chose to wear mine. This still makes me proud, especially since I greatly admire the legendary couturier. As with Riley Keough's wedding, the intense media attention, amplified by Lily being featured on magazine covers, helped draw attention to my business.

I think I helped Lily become the bride she wanted to be, but I have another secret: apparently, I also make mothers-to-be! The preparations for Lily's dress took almost a year. She had previously suffered devastating pregnancy losses, so during a fitting, I confided to her that I sew a little blue button in all my dresses, and that all my brides become pregnant. And that's just what happened. She was four or five months along on her wedding day. We had to adjust the dress a bit, but I'm used to that.

IV

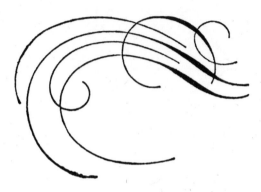

PLANNING
THE WEDDING

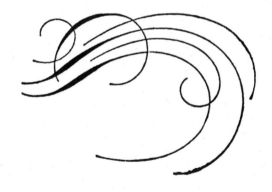

The Organized Bride

YOU'VE SPENT a long time imagining your ideal wedding, and now you're eager to bring your dreams to life. The good news is that planning a wedding doesn't have to involve panic and sleepless nights. Ordering hors d'oeuvres or creating a seating plan might not seem particularly exciting, but with a healthy dose of preparation, the months leading up to the wedding may actually be inspiring and reveal unexpected facets of yourself.

Unless you have a dedicated team of assistants, don't try too many unfamiliar things. Planning a day that tells your story doesn't mean you have to reinvent the very concept of marriage. Certain traditions have continued over the centuries precisely because they have given generations of brides a way to structure their ceremonies. Use the rituals that speak to you and adapt them to your own tastes.

As with many things, communication is key. Clearly explain your ideas to your vendors and to the other people supporting you but stay open to suggestions. And be honest with yourself. If you don't have enough time or money to plan a wedding exactly like the one in your childhood fantasies, you will have to make a few concessions—but that won't stop you from having a magical experience. Most importantly, stay focused on the direction you and your partner choose.

WEDDING PLANNER OR DIY?

Planning a wedding takes an enormous amount of energy, so having someone coordinate everything can be extremely valuable if you have more money than time. A wedding planner handles the thousand little problems that arise during any wedding and that you won't have time to deal with. Once again, everything depends on your budget and desires. Do whatever works, but if this luxury is available to you, embrace it with open arms.

Wedding planners have a tough job that deserves respect. Don't forget that they are people, not voice assistants; you can't call them in the middle of the night. Planning a wedding is both a job and an art that requires savoir faire.

The wedding planner's fee is usually based on the wedding budget. Rates vary, but typically they will ask for a fee amounting to between 5 and 15 percent of the total (which is very little, considering the amount of work and responsibility they have) or a fixed amount negotiated in advance.

You absolutely must get along well with your wedding planner. Before making a choice, meet with different candidates to discuss your ideas and be sure you understand one another. Use this as an opportunity to find out more about the services they offer, their fees, and the way they work. Ask them to tell you about a wedding they've planned.

Invitations and Thank-You Cards

IT IS CUSTOMARY to send guests a "save the date" note six to eight months before the wedding. This might be as simple as a text or something more personal, perhaps in the form of a handwritten note.

The wedding invitation should be mailed eight to ten weeks before the event. It sets the tone for the wedding, whether that means formal and traditional, or more casual and bohemian. Regardless, it should be well designed. Remember to specify the dress code—black tie and long dresses, for example—and if guests should anticipate a change of clothes to take them from day to evening. Include the names of the couple, date, time, location, whether the guest may come accompanied, and RSVP deadline and contact details. The invitation packet should also suggest transport options and accommodation near the venue. This information is all useful to guests and gives them a clear picture of what to expect.

Don't forget to make different invitations if some guests will only be invited to certain events, for example only the ceremony or the reception in the evening.

MY ADVICE

For a timelessly elegant invitation send one addressed with hand-lettered calligraphy, or a calligraphic font. Provide as many details as possible—I've noticed that guests appreciate receiving detailed guidance for a memorable weekend.

Since we're on the subject of writing, anticipate your thank-you cards, which should be sent within a month following the wedding. In the past, the tradition in France was to accompany the note with a photo of the newlyweds, but I find this a bit outdated. It's enough to send a few personal, handwritten words on pretty stationery that evokes the wedding theme.

The budget for wedding invitations will depend on the quality of the paper used and the way they are made, as well as your creativity and the amount of energy you are able to devote to them. If you go through a printer, ask for an estimate and make sure that they can offer what you want. Prices are typically costed per unit. If you prefer to do things yourself, be realistic about the amount of time this will take and the importance of finding the right materials.

Wedding
Favors

OFFERING A SMALL GIFT to your guests is a thoughtful gesture, a token of love and appreciation. But it has to be chosen carefully. According to French tradition, the bride is responsible for the favors, so they should reflect her personality. I suggest you imagine what gift you would like to receive. Forget baskets full of sugared almonds or tiny embroidered cushions; no one does that anymore. The ideal favor is something that your guests can easily take with them. Women often carry clutches or small handbags at weddings—a candle or potted cactus probably won't fit. Think of something small and portable.

Dance Card

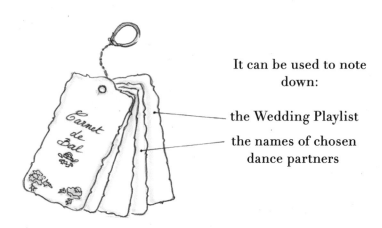

It can be used to note down:

the Wedding Playlist

the names of chosen dance partners

A good idea is to select a gift that guests can use on the wedding day itself. For example, if the ceremony takes place near the beach, you could place a large basket at the entrance to the reception venue full of flip-flops and *fouta* beach towels so guests can help themselves; if people's feet get sore as the festivities progress, they'll be very grateful. You could also hang a wall with straw hats your guests can choose to shade themselves from the sun. If the weather is cooler, they will be delighted to have shawls or light blankets to wrap up in come evening.

On the wedding day, guests love feeling like they are a part of something bigger, so giving them a gift is also an opportunity to bring them together. For smaller budgets, this could be as simple as a keepsake leather lanyard or silk ribbon placed near the dinner plates, or a small dance card where guests can write the names of the people they would like to pair up with during the evening. Some couples offer bottles of alcohol or olive oil, or small jars of sea salt, but these are a little cumbersome to carry and often end up forgotten on the tables. At the end of the night, the newlyweds find themselves with a hundred bottles of limoncello they don't know what to do with. Otherwise, small travel pouches for the women or tins of mints are inexpensive and can be quite useful all evening long.

The Wedding
Registry

EVEN IF YOU DON'T EXPECT your guests to shower you with gifts, you can be certain they're going to ask what you would like—or bring something, and if they do, beware of thirty-piece dinner sets and other bulky items you have no use for.

To avoid this, think ahead when it comes to gifts—it's actually fun to create a wedding registry. Rather than indulging in fantasies of luxury items like jewelry or watches, ask yourself what you and your partner really need, and suggest items covering a range of different prices. Your college-age cousin will probably be thrilled to offer you a little something if it's within her limited budget. If you have something very expensive in mind, or if you want to make a donation to a charity, you could also set up an online fund. Some couples ask for contributions to the honeymoon on the wedding registry, rather than heading home with fifteen salad spinners and three butter dishes. It comes down to what feels right to you and your partner.

There are many online wedding registry sites to choose from. Once you've created yours, send the link to people who ask for it—it's much more tactful than printing it directly on the invitation.

Reserving
the Venue

AS SOON AS you've picked out a theme or ambience for your wedding, start contacting and visiting venues that might be a good fit. In France, for example, châteaux are highly popular for weddings and get booked up months, if not years, in advance. If you have your heart set on a particularly sought-after venue, get in touch with the managers at least a year ahead—in some cases, even that is cutting it short.

If you're hiring an unusual venue, look into the conditions of use. Museums, for example, will have rules dictating how the space can be used, to avoid damaging their collections.

When you have a clear idea of the options available to you, rank them in order of preference and reserve the one that's first on the list. If it's not available, move right on to the next venue.

It may happen that a space you fell in love with remains out of reach. Make the best of it. You'll learn to love the next-best choice. What might seem like bad luck may actually be the beginning of a beautiful event.

You shouldn't ignore the connection you feel with a venue during a visit. But before rushing to book your favorite, ask yourself a few questions:

- Can this venue accommodate all of your guests? You don't want them crammed together, but the rooms shouldn't look empty either.
- Is it easy to get to? If your guests are arriving by car, is there enough parking?
- Is there accommodation in the area?
- Can you celebrate all night long? If not, is it possible to continue the party elsewhere?

- If it rains, is there somewhere for guests to take cover?
- And perhaps most importantly: Is reserving this space going to eat up your entire budget?

Make your decision based on your own priorities.

Ask the manager for precise information about the space:

- How many guests can the venue accommodate and what is the layout?
- Do they provide furniture, such as tables, chairs, and garden furniture? If not, can it be rented?
- Is it wheelchair accessible, etc.
- Is there accommodation on-site? If so, how many rooms are available and for what price?
- Are there any restrictions regarding hours or noise?
- Can they recommend vendors they have worked with?

Decoration

DESIGNING WEDDING DECOR is like undertaking a large painting: imagine that you're an artist and trust your eye.

The guiding principle for the *Parisienne* is balance. She gives the impression of having created a masterpiece effortlessly, when in reality she put a lot of thought into crafting a harmonious ensemble—not too much, not too little. If she chooses a Versailles-inspired theme, for example, she won't overdo it with gilded chandeliers and flowered patterns, or overt references to Marie Antoinette in everything from the plates to the menu. She prefers to scatter clues throughout that, when taken together, create an overall impression of grandeur.

Think about the ambience that you want to craft, adding and removing elements, playing with nuance, until you feel like you're achieving your vision. For the "wow" factor, pay attention to the details and watch out for false notes. If you've chosen a palette of bright, spring colors, don't use them on every surface; instead, make them a subtle unifying element.

Let yourself be inspired by the venue, rather than try to hide it. Coordinate your decor with what is already on-site. When you know the exact layout, aim to create distinct areas that flow naturally to suit a purpose: large open areas, like the dance floor, and more intimate corners for conversation.

It would be a shame to invest in lots of decorations if you're not going to use them again. To waste less and save more, look for pieces in second-hand shops or borrow from people you know. But beware of overusing mismatched elements; there's a fine line between finesse and flea market. Balance is key.

*If your reception venue doesn't provide fur-
niture, they can probably advise on a professional
rental company. They may have a choice of styles
that will suit the venue. Always plan for ten more
chairs than the number of guests.*

Don't forget about the importance of the floral design
to the overall effect. I've always preferred natural bouquets
to enormous, rigid constructions with every leaf and bloom
in place. Look for a variety of shapes and arrangements
depending on the purpose and setting: tables, windowsills,
bannisters etc. Choose seasonal flowers and use a florist near
the reception if possible.

Personally, I like small, square tables; they are often more convivial than large, round or oval tables, or long rectanglar ones, which may cause guests to be far apart and limit conversation. Guests also appreciate having the menu on the table. Reviewing it together is a way for them to break the ice.

If you work with a caterer, make sure you like the style of their place settings, and that it doesn't clash with the decor. Otherwise, why not dust off your grandmother's silverware, or use a combination of vintage finds?

"Forgotten" but Oh-So-Chic Spoons

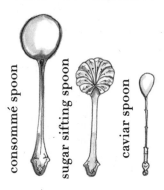

consommé spoon

sugar sifting spoon

caviar spoon

Beware of the proportions of centerpiece table decorations, which can isolate guests if they're too big. Better options are small candles and simple floral arrangements, or even olive branches or citrus fruits, if appropriate for the venue and season.

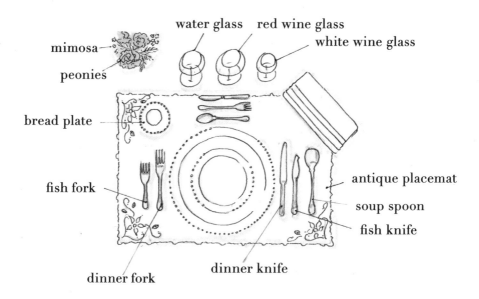

Traditional Place Setting

Bohemian Place Setting

Wedding Photographs

ALTHOUGH WITH SMARTPHONES today you will never be short of photos of your wedding, you will still want to hire an official photographer, if you can afford one. Photos taken by your friends are fun to look at but are unlikely to give you those special images that best capture your day.

But you don't have to hire a *wedding* photographer, per se. You can simply choose someone whose work you admire. Whatever you do, avoid clichéd images like awkwardly posed embraces or the newlyweds forming a heart with their hands. Choose poses that reflect you and your fiancé's personalities and truly express your feelings for one another.

Wedding photos are also important from a historical point of view because they speak to women's experiences and provide clues to their status at a given time. We can learn much from antique wedding photos: an image of a 1920s Parisian bride, for example, in a loose dress that reveals her ankles, hints at the nascent liberation of the times.

MY ADVICE

I like the idea of having a single, artistic photo, like in the old days; a lasting image—the one your grandchildren will look at. I don't think they'll be entranced by a close-up of your toenail polish. Try instead to create a truly different way of remembering your wedding, to keep it alive in your mind and heart, and to avoid accumulating thousands of photos that you'll never look at. If you accept this challenge, explain to your photographer that you only want one photo of you and your partner, one with your parents, one with your grandmother, and one with your friends. It's the best way to make memories that will last a lifetime.

Cortège de mariée et petites robes d'enfants
Collection Jeanne Lanvin

A Wedding Day
Emergency Kit

THE *PARISIENNE* PLANS ahead—she won't let a lack of organization ruin her big day. She wants to make the most of every moment. I suggest preparing a little bag of essential items to keep with you, just in case. Not only is it reassuring, but it also evokes the old tradition of the bride's trousseau. Put yours together about two weeks ahead of the wedding.

EMERGENCY KIT CHECKLIST

- Stain-removing wipes. Stains can happen in a flash. These wipes are very effective and reassuring to have on hand.
- A sewing kit with safety pins, a needle and thread, and a small pair of scissors. These will enable you to fix any issues with your dress, such as a broken strap.
- Wedding night lingerie. You never know exactly when you're going to wear it. Keeping it close allows you to enjoy the spontaneity of the moment.
- A second pair of shoes, preferably flats. Essential!
- Cooling foot spray. A bride almost never sits down, even during dinner, when she's expected to visit each table. Spritzing your feet during the evening is incredibly refreshing. Many of my brides say this item has been a lifesaver.
- Mints. You may get a dry mouth if you forget to hydrate because of stress, and champagne can cause bad breath. A bride needs to stay fresh until the very end.
- Deodorant. Smelling good is a basic but essential wedding-day objective. A bride goes through many emotions and is always on the move, so she's probably going to sweat.

- Tissues. The Parisian bride is very independent; she earns her living and depends on no one. But that doesn't prevent her from shedding a few tears during the ceremony.
- A pocket-sized facial spray. For cooling down just before applying mattifying powder, especially if the wedding takes place in summer.
- A compact with classic transparent setting powder. To prevent shine if you get hot or sweat.
- A good lip balm that doesn't transfer. For touching up lips during the day.
- Talcum powder. Apply it to your bust and waist before putting on your dress so it stays in place and doesn't stick.
- A beautiful white shirt or kimono to wear while getting ready. You'll likely be photographed, so your outfit is very important. And it will put you in the wedding mood.

Bridal Emergency Kit

lingerie for the wedding night

invisible lingerie for the wedding day

a pretty robe for hair and makeup

stain-removing wipes

talcum powder

shoes for the ceremony

a pair of flats

sewing kit

Planning
the Ceremony

THERE ARE A THOUSAND WAYS to celebrate your wedding ceremony, but what ultimately counts is the emotional investment and meaning you put into it. In fact, if you consider the ceremony to be just a formality, it doesn't have to be the focus of your wedding. But I think it's worthwhile to take this exceptional occasion to express how happy you are together, to declare your intentions of love, and to share your joy with those closest to you.

For both religious and secular ceremonies, you must work with the officiant to determine an order of events. Determining the right duration is also key to a successful celebration: it shouldn't be too short, but your guests will probably start nodding off if the sermon goes on for more than an hour. Make sure your guests are all comfortably seated and can see and hear you.

If allowed, bring a few decorative elements to brighten up the ceremony venue and create a connection with your wedding theme. The arch, a symbol of a couple's union, is a classic element of non-religious celebrations that comes in many forms. If the venue does not have its own arch or flower-covered arbor, you may be able to create one. Your imagination is the limit.

MY ADVICE

Write in capital red letters on your to-do list: "the morning of the wedding, call the person in charge of the rings to remind them to bring them."

If you decide to have a non-religious ceremony, you can involve family and friends. Contributions might include speeches, short musical performances, or poetry readings, as well as the vows—the possibilities are endless. But total freedom also implies careful planning to avoid gaps and awkward pauses. The officiant must remember the order of events and ensure smooth transitions.

And if you intend to hold the ceremony outdoors, come up with an alternative plan in case of bad weather.

COCKTAIL HOUR

After the ceremony, guests recover from the excitement as they mingle over drinks before the meal. This gives the newly-weds a little time to pause and chat with everyone present. The drink of choice might be a good champagne or the couple's favorite cocktail, accompanied by a few hors d'oeuvres.

Meals

A LOT RIDES on the reception dinner, the ultimate shared celebration, but planning doesn't have to give you an ulcer. In my opinion, the best strategy, if you have the budget, is to host several events, putting less stress on the main event: a rehearsal dinner the night before, a dinner the evening of the ceremony, a brunch the day after the wedding, and a final celebration with your closest friends.

THE REHEARSAL DINNER

This is the time to review everything before the wedding. Traditionally, it is organized by the groom's family. Guests include the wedding party, parents, and close friends — everyone who will play a particular role in the ceremony. In France this tradition is fading, but elsewhere it is a common part of the wedding celebrations. It can serve as a welcome party, particularly for people who have traveled long distances, where those closest to the couple gather and get to know each other in an intimate setting.

This doesn't have to be a seated dinner; you could plan a cocktail reception. In any case, your guests should have an early night to be ready for the next day. The rehearsal dinner is generally a convivial, joyful occasion appreciated by all.

THE RECEPTION DINNER

For the big day, you'll have to decide between a seated dinner and a cocktail reception. Parisians love to gather at the table and usually prefer assigned seats, but that requires organization and a certain budget to be successful. To keep the meal from dragging on, a seated reception requires a number of waitstaff. Another option is to serve only the main course at the table with a buffet for dessert. An interminable sit-down dinner isn't much fun for anyone and can ruin the ambiance.

The seating plan can also be a headache. French etiquette calls for alternating male and female guests and for following a protocol according to each person's status and age—don't make it a big deal. Instead, focus on the conversations that might arise between guests depending on their relationships or interests. (Naturally, if two people don't get along, they shouldn't be seated near one another.) The plan will gradually come together.

A cocktail reception can also be a success. Install several food stations, each featuring a different kind of food: bellota ham, mozzarella, seafood, fruit, candy, mini-burgers, fries, ice cream, for example. It's annoying to wait in line at a buffet, so if possible, have as many stations as you can. Select simple, seasonal, unprocessed foods as much as possible.

If you decide on a cocktail dinner, make sure there are areas where your guests can gather and sit down to eat.

If hiring a caterer, ask for a detailed quote that accounts for everything you need, including drinks, service, and tableware rental, if appropriate. Choose a professional who is familiar with large events and, if you can, contact people they've previously worked with to find out how things went.

Ask them to arrange a tasting of the menu options for you before making your decision. Remember to ask the caterer for examples of how they address specific dietary needs (a vegetarian option shouldn't be reduced to a two-leaf salad!).

Food and drink usually represent a quarter of the total wedding budget. Prices per head vary widely, depending on location and type of reception, so it is best to request quotes from several local caterers. Cocktail receptions tend to be more economical.

THE MENU

This is very personal, but I don't care for twelve-layer parfait-glasses, tumblers of green beans, and lukewarm steaks. Choose something you and your fiancé really like and want to share with your guests. Try to find food that reflects the region where you're getting married. Find out about the local specialties. And remember, trying to please everyone is a recipe for disaster. Chicken might be popular, but that doesn't mean I'll be serving it at my wedding.

The high point is the cake. A chic Parisian wedding cake doesn't necessarily have layers—in fact, it rarely does. The only requirement is that it be delicious. If your budget allows, I suggest ordering from an excellent pastry chef. But if you can't, a simple, homestyle cake made in an XL format also works well. The traditional French wedding cake is a *pièce montée*—a towering pyramid of sugar-dipped choux pastries. However, I recommend you choose a generous and beautiful cake instead; for a French touch, serve an oversized tarte Tropézienne or a tarte Tatin. Whatever you decide, remember, it's a treat, and the highlight of the evening. Cutting the cake is the cue to kick off the dancing.

Entertainment

IN GENERAL, avoid games that involve making fools of your guests or screaming into a microphone—that's a surefire way to destroy the magic of the moment. A few moving speeches, some music, and a lot of dancing is enough to make for a memorable night.

KEEPING THE KIDS ENTERTAINED

If you choose to host children, hire someone to lead activities for them, including a couple of babysitters who will look after the little ones all day. During the ceremony, place caretakers strategically so they can attend to the needs of the children. Evening activities could include making flower crowns, face painting, a treasure hunt, and other games.

If you can, set up an area where children can rest—this gift to your friends will enable them to fully enjoy the party.

MUSIC

Music is an essential element of a wedding: a soundtrack can really set the tone. I'm a fan of live music—it's a gamechanger. Put a quartet in a church and you're sure to have a magical event. You could also have musicians play at the end of the ceremony, during the cocktail hour. Quiet, live music that continues through dinner creates a wonderful mood.

Hiring a DJ for the dance portion of the reception can be risky, so make your choice with the utmost care. A tacky DJ can ruin a wedding. If you want to cut your budget, cut out the DJ. Instead, gather your friends ahead of time and make playlists full of songs that will get everyone dancing.

MY ADVICE

Invite your guests to put together twenty-minute sets. Tell them you would love to have them choose some of the party music—it's a good way of getting your friends involved and creating a few nice surprises for yourself.

THE FIRST DANCE

Consider choosing a dance related to your theme. If your wedding is in a Roaring Twenties style, a few nods to the Charleston will only add to the mood. Whatever you decide on, make sure you're comfortable; a simple waltz can be wonderful if you put your heart into it.

SPEECHES

My only advice regarding speeches: stay in control. Plan everything ahead of time so there is nothing awkward or embarrassing.

This is the moment to be a control freak. Avoid blunders, like your cousin talking about your first set of braces or your best friend recalling the number of lovers you had in college. I would say that a maximum of four or five speeches over the course of the evening is plenty.

THE NEXT DAY

The pressure lifts the day after the wedding. The newlyweds are more relaxed and can fully enjoy the moment. You could host a late-morning brunch and a soirée later. Again, it all depends on your budget. You could also ask your friends to chip in for the final celebration.

When I got married at the age of twenty-six, we were fortunate enough to have our post-wedding party on a private beach in the south of France. Only our closest friends were there, and it remains my fondest memory. The wedding day itself was wonderful, but the day after was the ultimate highlight—a moment that, in a way, was mine alone.

Spotlight on Lady Gaga

THE ICONIC LADY GAGA hasn't yet tied the knot, but she has worn many of my creations, including a wedding dress she wore for a major milestone in her career: the opening ceremony of the European Games in Baku, Azerbaijan.

Lady Gaga has always had a distinctive style: eccentric, even decadent, and boundary-pushing. The first time she contacted me, I didn't see how our worlds could connect. And then I understood: she is an extremely sensitive person, with an almost childlike sense of romanticism. I think she likes my dresses for the stories they tell, regardless of whether or not they are wedding gowns. In my humble way, that's what I try to do: create dresses that matter, for moments that matter.

I have to admit that my heart raced when I saw her walk barefoot across that huge stage, majestic and enveloped in my white chiffon wedding dress. Then she sat behind a piano piled with flowers to perform John Lennon's "Imagine." It is one of the most seminal, intense moments in my career. I could never have imagined such a beautiful scene, and I was a small part of it. Lady Gaga is probably the only one of my clients who has never asked for the slightest alteration to my design, and I have always been touched by her thoughtfulness. For this event, I had imagined her wearing heels, but she decided to go barefoot, and didn't ask for a single change to the dress. And while it is clear in the video that the gown was too long, when she swept up the train in her hand, the sight was even more magical.

This incredible artist gave me the marvelous impression that she understood my dresses down to the smallest detail and respected them as though they were individuals. Lady Gaga has always granted me her trust and this gift.

V

HAPPILY
EVER AFTER

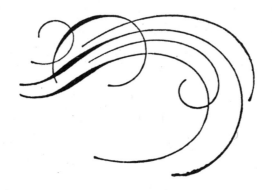

The Honeymoon

A HONEYMOON is often the trip of a lifetime, and you should plan it while you're organizing the wedding. If you postpone your departure, there's a good chance you'll never go.

After the magic of the wedding, you might get a case of the wedding blues. You will have received an enormous amount of love, and the comedown can be harsh. So find your partner and savor the moment. If you can, take at least a week to ten days and do something out of the ordinary that you both enjoy. The buddymoon, a new trend from South Africa, is a nice alternative that involves going away with a few friends to celebrate, on an island, for example.

In any case, I think it's important to mark the occasion in a way that suits you. You don't have to head to Bora-Bora for two months; what matters is that you share a special moment with your partner.

It's also fun to pack for your honeymoon before your wedding. What swimsuits will you bring? Should you take sarongs or pretty dresses? Planning ahead will give you a post-wedding objective to focus on. With your honeymoon to look forward to, you'll know the celebration doesn't end with the wedding. For peace of mind, and to make sure you don't forget anything, I recommend that you finish packing for the trip two weeks before the wedding.

MY ADVICE

Your wedding registry is a good place to ask for a set of good-quality luggage that will last you a lifetime.

PACKING LIST FOR
A WEEKLONG BEACH HONEYMOON

- Two outfits per day: one for daytime and one for evening
- Swimsuits
- Sarongs
- Beach dresses
- Flowy "sundown" dresses
- A pair of flat leather sandals that goes with everything
- A pair of flipflops
- A pair of pretty heels
- A small clutch or handbag for the evening
- A small bag for the beach

Now the real journey begins: life as a couple, as a partnership, and as a family. What form will your love take? How can you make it last 'til death do you part?

The Rest of Your Life

IS THERE A SECRET to a successful relationship and lasting love?

I'm not an expert, but throughout my life, and thanks to my work, I have had the opportunity to observe and speak with thousands of couples. This has shown me that certain dynamics seem to make for a solid, even indestructible, foundation. Some couples appear to have found a perfect balance. I've identified four archetypes for long-lasting love, but of course there are others out there.

 ## MICHAEL AND DIANE: ADMIRATION AND RESPECT

He is eighty and she is seventy-eight, and they split their time between England and South Africa.

Every day, without exception, he tells her that he loves her. They constantly shower each other with compliments like "you're handsome," "you're beautiful," and "you're talented." They come together for countless small rituals. In the evening, they share a glass of white wine; in the morning, he goes for a swim while she writes at her desk (she's an author of children's books) and when he returns, it's as if they've been apart for days. I believe that she has become a greater artist because he reassures her. As for him, he's a happy man because she surprises him. I have never seen the slightest hint of mockery or sarcasm between them— never, under any circumstances. It can be so easy to take a snipe at one another, especially in social situations, but the gestures and looks they exchange are only ever filled with kindness.

Hand in hand, they evolve together while retaining their unique identities. People refer to them as "Mike and Diane," but really there is a Diane and a Michael, and each is a distinct individual. You can develop a relationship with her or with him, but not so much with the both of them.

Perhaps that's one of the secrets: knowing how to show your love for one another while shielding your relationship from the outside world. Helping it to grow independently and privately, almost in secret, and always with kindness.

MARIE-CHRISTINE AND ALAIN: IN SYNC

I've had many occasions to observe this couple—my mother and her "companion" (as she likes to call him). They live in the south of France but in separate homes.

They met relatively late in life, at the age of seventy-one. Both have troubled romantic pasts, but they were ready to love at that moment and decided to remain open to the unknown.

They are both very independent, and yet, from the very beginning of their relationship, they have been connected at the hip. What unites them is a similar rhythm and enormous curiosity. They see each other on weekends and vacation together.

They buoy one another up, spur one another on. If one of them feels their appetite for the world waning, the other whets it again. The danger for couples lies in succumbing to a predictable routine: going outside when the weather is nice and staying in when it's cold. They, on the other hand, are very active—you could even say they have a hard time staying still. They're curious about everything and are constantly exploring new interests, cultures, and travels. They discover things together and that nourishes their relationship. Since they don't live together, they miss each other and are eager to meet again. My mother often tells me that she's too busy — there are so many books to read, villages to visit, and movies to watch. This thirst for discovery and knowledge keeps both mind and body very youthful. My mother looks exceptionally good for her age, yet she's never used anything but budget moisturizer. She is deeply connected to herself, to nature, and, now, with the love of her life. And I haven't given up on the possibility of seeing them get married one day.

Perhaps that's one of the secrets: create a feeling of absence by living apart, so that you look forward to each other's company and sustain the joy of discovering new things together every day.

VICTOIRE AND CHARLES: A FOUNDATION OF SHARED VALUES

This is THE couple of my generation. Victoire and Charles are my oldest friends. They've been together since they were sixteen and have been passionately in love for thirty years. What do they have in common? They share the same family values. If one of their mothers falls ill, she moves into the house — neither of them questions this. It is part of the contract their love is built on and it is extremely precious. Their parents and children are at the center of everything, the bedrock of their relationship.

They share everyday life and always have new projects underway. The environment they have created is so stable that it allows them to develop individually, but also to help many others around them. Many people struggle with the occasional feeling of loneliness, but these two remain unaffected by it. Their relationship is indestructible because they are united. They are the polestar for couples, pointing the way.

They never let problems gain a foothold; they talk about things right away, taking action to find solutions quickly. Victoire once told me, "Marriage shouldn't be a struggle; you should be able to imagine making your way calmly through life."

Perhaps that's one of the secrets: sharing the same values and plans from the beginning, being in tune with each other, wanting the same kind of life, and never letting small problems take root.

 SERENA AND JAMIE: FUN WITH AN ELEMENT OF SURPRISE

I've observed this couple, my Finnish friends, both at home and in social situations.

She is an artist and he is a photographer. They each have a totally unique and inspiring world. What has always struck me is their shared, almost childlike zest for fun. They change clothes several times a day: in a way, they are playing dress up, and it's full of joy.

In their traditional *mökki*, a cabin in the Finnish woods where everything is intimately connected to nature, Serena spends a lot of time making the interior cozy by practicing hygge, the Scandinavian art of arranging objects, candles, or flowers picked in the garden. But these arrangements are never permanent: she changes her decor several times a week. Nothing is set in stone, and she makes modifications according to the light or the seasons, or even the people she welcomes into her home.

As for Jamie, he might change his hat several times a day and put on an eccentric outfit before he goes out to gather mushrooms, much like a child who dons a pirate's hat to fight an imaginary battle.

Deep down, I don't think they've ever gotten used to each other, in the sense that they've never let familiarity set in. They constantly surprise each other through this idea of metamorphosis and their own aesthetic vision.

Perhaps that's one of the secrets: keep putting flowers on the table, wearing hats, and asking "What can we play?" each day.

THE ART OF AGING GRACEFULLY

Choosing to marry someone implies choosing to grow old with them.

Growing old, continuing to love myself and my body, and having it be loved despite the passing years, has always been a concern of mine. I find it rather terrifying. I still don't have all the answers, and I keep talking about it to those around me. But being gentle and showing kindness toward yourself and others seems to be one path that leads to acceptance. We should stop judging ourselves. Over the years, I've come to realize that it isn't how others see us that is most difficult to endure, but the way we see ourselves—we are our own harshest critics. Looking at yourself differently, with tolerance and tenderness, is a good first step.

What can we do to resist the pressure to show the world a youthful face when we aren't young anymore? I haven't tried medical solutions or cosmetic surgery myself, but through my work I have seen everything that's new and revolutionary in the field, including techniques to enlarge breasts or buttocks, liposuction, nose jobs, fillers and Botox, tensile threads, and dermabrasion.

The techniques used in aesthetic medicine have evolved considerably over the years. If a woman has a complex about something—even if no one else sees it—surgery may change the way she sees herself and thus change her life.

But the greatest danger, in my opinion, is addiction. I have seen some of my friends and brides who can no longer go without that shot of adrenaline. Beyond feeling beautiful, it's the surge of self-confidence that's so intoxicating. It clouds their judgment. In such cases, sometimes even their loved ones fail to bring them back to reality.

In the near future, I can imagine a new kind of profession developing: "beauty regulators." These individuals would be guardians of their clients' beauty by remaining honest with them. In a way, this is what I do already. I advise brides of all ages and, most importantly, when they can no longer tell what looks beautiful on them, I try to tell them when something is too much or when it's time to leave well enough alone.

The real challenge in the years to come will be determining how to grow old gracefully. Beauty is an eternal concept, but when it is unclear what stage a person is in their life, a certain type of elegance is lost.

When I asked my grandmother, who I am lucky to still have with me, what her secret to happiness was, she said, "You know, my dear, I dance in my head." She was ninety-four at the time, and even though her body could no longer dance, she found another way to continue doing it. I will treasure these words forever.

Certain women are my role models, my guiding lights, even if I know I must write my own story. Audrey Hepburn worked as ambassador for UNICEF in her sixties; she was so radiant during that period. Photos of her with the children she met show her inner beauty emanating from within.

Simone Veil, who spent her life fighting for women's rights, remains an example of elegance, beauty, self-restraint, and strength for many French women. My mother, who dedicated her life to society's most disadvantaged, is lovelier than ever. And, at the age of seventy-five, she decided to explore all of France's most beautiful villages with her companion, while continuing to care for her friends and grandchildren.

Aging well means accepting that each stage of life is beautiful in its own way. Now *that* is wisdom. Intelligence also means understanding the passing of time. Know how to lean into life's curves, to choose your own direction and to avoid wrong turns—but if you take one, being willing to turn around and find your rhythm again—getting back in tune with yourself and your age, and with the period of life you're traveling through.

Conclusion

TODAY, WEDDINGS don't have to be standardized or formal. Couples are shattering conventions. You can get married in a thousand and one ways: at the age of twenty-five or seventy; in a church, a synagogue, a meadow, or on the coast; in a simple ceremony at the city hall or by planning a huge celebration; to a man or a woman; to your best friend; with two guests or five hundred; for a huge budget or a modest one; with your whole family present, just your witnesses, or the entire village; wearing a veil or flowers in your hair; with sneakers on your feet; in winter or in summer, in the countryside or the mountains, or in Paris.

Weddings tell the story of human beings, of their doubts and their bonds, and even if this event must evolve with time or take on a different name, the tradition of celebrating love absolutely must prevail: reveling in two beings who meet and decide to share their lives, to create a new world together.

I'd like to get married again, but I don't yet know what path I'm going to take. May your curiosity and your creativity remain alive, and continue to let yourself be surprised. Remember to celebrate and acknowledge the sacred nature of this event, and, in the process, capture a fragment of eternity.

Timeline for Planning Your Wedding

AFTER THE ENGAGEMENT
- Gather inspiration
- Throw an engagement party, if you feel like it
- Discuss a budget with your friends and family, and make estimates
- Make a first draft of the guest list
- Look for reception venues you like and contact the owners for more information
- Pick a date, according to the availability of the reception venue

6–8 MONTHS BEFORE THE BIG DAY
- Finalize the guest list
- Send a "save the date" note
- Choose your wedding party
- Contact the venue where you want to hold the ceremony to get details about the process and timeline
- Reserve the ceremony and reception venues
- Research transport options and accommodation for your guests
- Draw up an hour-by-hour schedule for the wedding day
- Contact different vendors, explain to them exactly what you want, and compare quotes
- Design your wedding invitations
- Choose your dress

2–5 MONTHS BEFORE THE BIG DAY

- Send your wedding invitations
- Decide on outfits for the wedding party, including the flower girl and ring bearer
- Order or start making wedding favors
- Choose your wedding bands
- Depending on the wedding venue, pick out furniture and decor, and think about how you will collect and transport items to the site
- Plan the format or the ceremony
- Attend a tasting with potential caterers
- Select vendors and work with them to determine a menu, a photography style, floral design, and other details
- Plan evening entertainment
- Establish back-up plans
- Take care of paperwork
- Set up your wedding registry

THE FINAL WEEKS LEADING UP TO THE BIG DAY

- Attend your bachelorette party
- Write your vows
- Practice the first dance
- If children are invited, find trustworthy babysitters
- Double-check that your vendors have all the information they need and remember the date
- Resolve any outstanding issues
- Order the cake
- Order your bouquet
- Make a list of bridal party duties
- Go for a final dress fitting

- Find out when you can access the venue to decorate and to stage flower arrangements and furniture, if necessary
- Relax and pamper yourself

THE BIG DAY

- Make the most of it!

ACKNOWLEDGMENTS

I wish to thank Sophie de Closets for her trust and friendship; Anne Akrich for her sense of humor and the precision with which she chose the words for this guide; and Elsa Huisman for always believing in me and for her friendship that I hold so dear.

Editorial Directors
KATE MASCARO and JULIE ROUART
Editors
HELEN ADEDOTUN and YAËL RUSÉ
Administration Manager
DELPHINE MONTAGNE
Translation from the French
KATE ROBINSON
Design
SARAH MARTINON
Copyediting
LINDSAY PORTER
Typesetting
CLAUDE-OLIVIER FOUR
Proofreading
NICOLE FOSTER
Production
ÉLODIE CONJAT
Color Separation
LES ARTISANS DU REGARD, PARIS
Printed in Belgium by
GRAPHIUS

Originally published in French as *Oui!*
Mes secrets pour réaliser le mariage
de vos rêves
© Éditions Flammarion, Paris, 2024

English-language edition
© Éditions Flammarion, Paris, 2025

editions.flammarion.com
@flammarioninternational
25 26 27 3 2 1
ISBN: 978-2-08- 044730-2
Legal Deposit: 02/2025

This book is typeset in Didot and printed sustainably on PEFC-certified Holmen Book
Extra paper with vegetable-based inks by an ISO 14001- and Ecovadis-certified printer.